Vegetarian Barbecues

Vegetarian Barbecues

SUE ASHWORTH

||| •PARRAGON• |||

First published in Great Britain in 1995 by
Parragon Book Service Ltd
Unit 13-17
Avonbridge Trading Estate
Atlantic Road
Avonmouth
Bristol BS11 9QD

ISBN 1 85813 916 3

Produced by Haldane Mason, London

Printed in Italy

Acknowledgements:

Art Direction: Ron Samuels
Editor: Joanna Swinnerton
Series Design: Pedro & Frances Prá-Lopez/Kingfisher Design
Page Design: Somewhere Creative
Photography and styling: Iain Bagwell
Home Economist: Sue Ashworth
Assistant Home Economist: Yvonne Melville

Photographs on pages 6, 20, 34, 48 and 62 are reproduced by permission of ZEFA Picture Library (UK) Ltd.

The photographer would like to thank Ceramica Blue and Webber Barbecues for the loan of props.

Note:

Cup measurements in this book are for American cups. Tablespoons are assumed to be 15 ml. Unless otherwise stated, milk is assumed to be full-fat, eggs are standard size 2 and pepper is freshly ground black pepper.

Contents

CHAPTER ONE

Dips, Sauces & Marinades

In this chapter, you will find some delicious ideas for tasty dips, a spicy barbecue sauce, rich marinades and lively dressings – those all-important details that complete the barbecue and make the food taste superb. There are some great barbecue basics here, designed to excite the palate and to add to the flavour of the finished food.

One point that is crucial to the whole idea of outdoor eating is that although the food should be simple and easy to prepare, it should still taste wonderful. All the ideas in this chapter have been developed with that aim in mind. Here you will find recipes that are quick to put together, taking only moments to assemble.

When marinating food, it is a good idea to prepare it several hours before the barbecue, so that it has plenty of time to soak up the flavours of the marinade. The same principle applies to the sauces, dips and dressings too, as the longer the ingredients are combined, the more the flavours will develop and mellow. Besides, the earlier these are prepared, the less you will have to do at the barbecue!

Opposite: *A simple dressing made with fresh herbs, spices, aromatic oils, sharp vinegars and a range of fruit and vegetable ingredients will add an invaluable flavour to your barbecue food.*

STEP 1

STEP 2

STEP 3

STEP 4

BUTTERED NUT & LENTIL DIP

This tasty dip is very easy to make. It is perfect to have at barbecues, as it gives your guests something to nibble while they are waiting for their cooked food.

SERVES 4

60 g/2 oz/¼ cup butter
1 small onion, chopped
90 g/3 oz/⅓ cup red lentils
300 ml /½ pint/ 1¼ cups vegetable stock
60 g/2 oz/½ cup blanched almonds
60 g/2 oz/½ cup pine kernels (nuts)
½ tsp ground coriander
½ tsp ground cumin
½ tsp freshly grated root ginger
1 tsp chopped fresh coriander (cilantro)
salt and pepper
*sprigs of fresh coriander (cilantro) to
  garnish*

TO SERVE:
fresh vegetable crudités
bread sticks

1 Melt half the butter in a saucepan and fry the onion gently until golden brown.

2 Add the lentils and vegetable stock. Bring to the boil, then reduce the heat and simmer gently, uncovered, for about 25–30 minutes until the lentils are tender. Drain well.

3 Melt the remaining butter in a small frying pan (skillet). Add the almonds and pine kernels (nuts) and fry them gently until golden brown. Remove from the heat.

4 Put the lentils, almonds and pine kernels (nuts), with any remaining butter, into a blender or food processor. Add the ground coriander, cumin, ginger and fresh coriander (cilantro). Blend until smooth, about 15–20 seconds. Alternatively, push the lentils through a sieve (strainer) to purée them and mix with the finely chopped nuts, spices and herbs.

5 Season the dip with salt and pepper and garnish with sprigs of fresh coriander (cilantro). Serve with fresh vegetable crudités and bread sticks.

VARIATIONS

Green or brown lentils can be used, but they will take longer to cook than red lentils.

If you wish, substitute peanuts for the almonds to make a more economical version.

Ground ginger can be used instead of fresh root ginger – substitute ½ teaspoon and add it to the food processor or blender with the other spices.

STEP 1

STEP 2

STEP 3

STEP 4

TZATZIKI WITH PITTA (POCKET) BREADS & BLACK OLIVE DIP

Tzatziki is a Greek dish, made with natural yogurt, mint and cucumber. It tastes superb with warm pitta (pocket) bread and the black olive dip provides a delicious contrast of flavour.

SERVES 4

½ cucumber
250 g/8 oz/1 cup thick natural yogurt
1 tbsp chopped fresh mint
salt and pepper
4 pitta (pocket) breads

DIP:
2 garlic cloves, crushed
125 g/4 oz/¾ cup pitted black olives
4 tbsp olive oil
2 tbsp lemon juice
1 tbsp chopped fresh parsley

TO GARNISH:
sprigs of fresh mint
sprigs of fresh parsley

1 To make the tzatziki, peel the cucumber and chop roughly. Sprinkle it with salt and leave it to stand for 15–20 minutes. Rinse with cold water and drain well.

2 Mix the cucumber, yogurt and mint together. Season with salt and pepper and transfer to a serving bowl. Cover and chill for 20–30 minutes.

3 To make the dip, put the crushed garlic and olives into a blender or

food processor and blend for 15–20 seconds. Alternatively, chop them very finely.

4 Add the olive oil, lemon juice and parsley to the blender or food processor and blend for a few more seconds. Alternatively, mix with the chopped garlic and olives and mash together. Season with salt and pepper.

5 Wrap the pitta (pocket) breads in foil and place over the barbecue for 2–3 minutes, turning once to warm through. Alternatively, heat in the oven or under the grill (broiler). Cut into pieces and serve with the tzatziki and black olive dip, garnished with sprigs of fresh mint and parsley.

TIPS

Sprinkling the cucumber with salt draws out some of its moisture, making it crisper. If you are in a hurry, you can omit this procedure.

Use green olives instead of black ones if you prefer.

HEAVENLY GARLIC DIP WITH CRUDITÉS

Anyone who loves garlic will adore this dip – it is very potent! Keep it warm over the hot coals to one side of the barbecue, and dip raw vegetables or hunks of French bread into it.

STEP 1

SERVES 4

2 bulbs garlic
6 tbsp olive oil
1 small onion, chopped finely
2 tbsp lemon juice
3 tbsp tahini (sesame seed paste)
2 tbsp chopped fresh parsley
salt and pepper

TO SERVE:
fresh vegetable crudités
French bread or warmed pitta
    (pocket) breads

1 Separate the bulbs of garlic into individual cloves. Place them on a baking sheet and roast in a preheated oven at 200°C/400°F/Gas mark 6 for 8–10 minutes. Leave to cool for a few minutes.

2 Peel the garlic cloves, then chop them finely.

3 Heat the olive oil in a saucepan or frying pan (skillet) and add the chopped garlic and chopped onion. Fry gently for 8–10 minutes until softened. Remove the pan from the heat.

4 Mix the lemon juice, tahini and parsley into the garlic mixture. Season to taste with salt and pepper. Transfer to a small heatproof bowl and keep warm at one side of the barbecue.

5 Serve with fresh vegetable crudités, chunks of French bread or warm pitta (pocket) breads.

STEP 2

STEP 3

SMOKED GARLIC

If you come across smoked garlic, use it in this recipe – it tastes wonderful. There is no need to roast the smoked garlic, so omit the first step.

This dip can also be used to baste kebabs and vegetarian burgers.

STEP 4

STEP 1

STEP 2

STEP 3

STEP 4

TASTY BARBECUE SAUCE

Just the thing for brushing on to vegetable kebabs and burgers, this sauce takes only minutes to make.

SERVES 4

30 g/1 oz/2 tbsp butter or margarine
1 garlic clove, crushed
1 onion, chopped finely
400 g/13 oz can of chopped tomatoes
1 tbsp dark muscovado sugar
1 tsp hot chilli sauce
15 g/¹⁄₂ oz/1–2 gherkins
1 tbsp capers, drained
salt and pepper

1 Melt the butter or margarine in a saucepan and fry the garlic and onion until well browned, about 8–10 minutes.

2 Add the chopped tomatoes, sugar and chilli sauce. Bring to the boil, then reduce the heat and simmer gently for 20–25 minutes, until thick and pulpy.

3 Chop the gherkins and capers finely.

4 Add the chopped gherkins and capers to the sauce, stirring well to mix. Cook the sauce for a further 2 minutes.

5 Taste the sauce and season with a little salt and pepper. Use as a baste for vegetarian kebabs and burgers, or as an accompaniment to other barbecued food.

TIPS

To make sure that the sauce has a good colour, it is important to brown the onions really well to begin with.

When fresh tomatoes are cheap and plentiful, they can be used instead of canned ones. Peel and chop 500 g/1 lb, and add them as before.

Substitute chilli powder instead of chilli sauce, according to taste. If you prefer a milder version of barbecue sauce, leave it out altogether.

STEP 1

STEP 2

STEP 3

STEP 4

CITRUS & FRESH HERB MARINADES

Choose one of these marinades to give a marvellous flavour to the food that is to be barbecued. Or just use them for brushing on to the food while it cooks over the hot coals.

EACH DRESSING SERVES 4

ORANGE, CHIVE & MARJORAM:
1 orange
120 ml/4 fl oz/¹/₂ cup olive oil
4 tbsp dry white wine
4 tbsp white wine vinegar
1 tbsp snipped fresh chives
1 tbsp chopped fresh marjoram
salt and pepper

THAI-SPICED LIME & CORIANDER
(CILANTRO):
1 stalk lemon grass
finely grated rind and juice of 1 lemon
4 tbsp sesame oil
2 tbsp light soy sauce
pinch of ground ginger
1 tbsp chopped fresh coriander (cilantro)
salt and pepper

BASIL, LEMON & OREGANO:
finely grated rind of 1 lemon
4 tbsp lemon juice
1 tbsp balsamic vinegar
2 tbsp red wine vinegar
2 tbsp virgin olive oil
1 tbsp chopped fresh oregano
1 tbsp chopped fresh basil
salt and pepper

1 To make the Orange, Chive & Marjoram Marinade, remove the rind from the orange with a zester, or grate it finely, then squeeze the juice.

2 Mix the orange rind and juice with all the remaining ingredients in a small bowl, whisking together to combine. Season with salt and pepper.

3 To make the Thai-spiced Lime & Coriander (Cilantro) Marinade, bruise the lemon grass by crushing it with a rolling pin. Mix the remaining ingredients together and add the lemon grass.

4 To make the Basil, Lemon & Oregano Marinade, whisk all the ingredients together in a small bowl. Season with salt and pepper.

5 Keep the marinades covered with clingfilm (plastic wrap) or store in screw-top jars, ready for using as marinades or bastes.

STEP 1

STEP 2

STEP 3

STEP 4

THREE FAVOURITE DRESSINGS

You can rely on any one of these delicious dressings to bring out the very best in your salads.

EACH DRESSING SERVES 4

*WHOLEGRAIN MUSTARD & CIDER
    VINEGAR DRESSING:*
120 ml/4 fl oz/¹/₂ cup olive oil
4 tbsp cider vinegar
2 tsp wholegrain mustard
¹/₂ tsp caster (superfine) sugar
salt and pepper

GARLIC & PARSLEY DRESSING:
1 small garlic clove
1 tbsp fresh parsley
150 ml /¹/₄ pint/²/₃ cup single (light) cream
4 tbsp natural yogurt
1 tsp lemon juice
pinch of caster (superfine) sugar
salt and pepper

*RASPBERRY & HAZELNUT
    VINAIGRETTE:*
4 tbsp raspberry vinegar
4 tbsp light olive oil
4 tbsp hazelnut oil
¹/₂ tsp caster (superfine) sugar
2 tsp chopped fresh chives
salt and pepper

1 To make the Wholegrain Mustard & Cider Vinegar Dressing, whisk all the ingredients together in a small bowl.

2 To make the Garlic & Parsley Dressing, crush the garlic clove and chop the parsley finely.

3 Mix the garlic and parsley with the remaining ingredients. Whisk together until combined, then cover and chill for 30 minutes.

4 To make the Raspberry & Hazelnut Vinaigrette, whisk all the ingredients together until combined.

5 Keep the dressings covered with clingfilm (plastic wrap) or sealed in screw-top jars. Chill until ready for use.

PERFECT COMBINATIONS

Wholegrain Mustard & Cider Vinegar Dressing is excellent with a tomato salad. Garlic & Parsley Dressing tastes delicious as a coating for potato salad and Raspberry & Hazelnut Vinaigrette makes a superb dressing for mixed salad leaves (greens).

CHAPTER TWO

Filled Things

Easy-to-eat food is essential for barbecues. More often than not, barbecued food is eaten while standing up and moving around, and it is tricky trying to balance a plate, eat from it, hold a glass and have a conversation at the same time! Hopefully, the ideas in this section will help to make the balancing act a little easier.

By providing a range of filled foods such as pitta (pocket) and naan breads, baguettes, jacket potatoes, burger buns and the occasional stuffed vegetable, you will be offering self-contained food that is easy to eat and enjoy – a movable feast! What's more, these ideas are perfect for children, who never seem to sit still for a moment.

The choices offered in this section are deliciously different and very tasty. Try, for instance, the Naan Bread with Curried Vegetable Kebabs – a mouthwatering recipe for barbecued kebabs brushed with a spicy combination of coriander, cumin and chilli powder blended in natural yogurt. Served with Indian bread warmed over the hot coals, it really is a winner.

Opposite: *The setting sun provides a perfect backdrop for an unforgettable barbecue.*

STEP 1

STEP 2

STEP 3

STEP 4

FILLED JACKET POTATOES

Cook these potatoes conventionally, then wrap them in foil and keep them warm at the edge of the barbecue, ready to fill with a choice of three inspired mixtures.

EACH DRESSING SERVES **4**

4 large or 8 medium baking potatoes

MEXICAN SWEETCORN RELISH:
250 g/8 oz can of sweetcorn, drained
$^1/_2$ red (bell) pepper, cored, deseeded and chopped finely
5 cm/2 inch piece cucumber, chopped finely
$^1/_2$ tsp chilli powder
salt and pepper

BLUE CHEESE, CELERY & CHIVE FILLING:
125 g/4 oz/$^1/_2$ cup cream cheese
125 g/4 oz/$^1/_2$ cup natural fromage frais
125 g/4 oz Danish blue cheese, cut into cubes
1 celery stick, chopped finely
2 tsp snipped fresh chives
celery salt and pepper

MUSHROOMS IN SPICY TOMATO SAUCE:
30 g/1 oz/2 tbsp butter or margarine
250 g/8 oz button mushrooms
150 g/5 oz/$^2/_3$ cup natural yogurt
1 tbsp tomato purée (paste)
2 tsp mild curry powder
salt and pepper
paprika or chilli powder, or chopped fresh herbs, to garnish

1 Scrub the potatoes and prick them with a fork. Bake in a preheated oven at 200°C/400°F/Gas Mark 6 for about 1 hour, until just tender.

2 To make the Mexican Sweetcorn Relish, put half the sweetcorn into a bowl. Put the remainder into a blender or food processor for 10–15 seconds or chop and mash roughly by hand. Add the puréed sweetcorn to the sweetcorn kernels with the (bell) pepper, cucumber and chilli powder. Season to taste.

3 To make the Blue Cheese, Celery & Chive Filling, mix the cream cheese and fromage frais together until smooth. Add the blue cheese, celery and chives. Season with pepper and celery salt.

4 To make the Mushrooms in Spicy Tomato Sauce, melt the butter or margarine in a small frying pan (skillet). Add the mushrooms and cook gently for 3–4 minutes. Remove from the heat and stir in the yogurt, tomato purée (paste) and curry powder. Season to taste.

5 Wrap the cooked potatoes in foil and keep warm at the edge of the barbecue. Serve the fillings sprinkled with paprika or chilli powder or herbs.

STEP 1

STEP 2

STEP 3

STEP 4

MELTING CHEESE & ONION BAGUETTES

Part-baked baguettes are split and filled with a tasty cheese and onion mixture, then wrapped in foil and cooked over the barbecue to make them warm, crisp and delicious.

SERVES 4

4 part-baked baguettes
2 tbsp tomato relish
60 g/2 oz/¼ cup butter
8 spring onions (scallions), trimmed and
    chopped finely
125 g/4 oz/½ cup cream cheese
125 g/4 oz/1 cup Cheddar cheese, grated
1 tsp snipped fresh chives
pepper

TO SERVE:
mixed salad leaves (greens)
fresh herbs

1 Split the part-baked baguettes in half lengthways, without cutting right through. Spread a little tomato relish on each split baguette.

2 Melt the butter in a frying pan (skillet) and add the spring onions (scallions). Fry them gently until softened and golden. Remove from the heat and leave to cool slightly.

3 Beat the cream cheese in a mixing bowl to soften it. Mix in the spring onions (scallions), with any remaining butter. Add the grated cheese and snipped chives, and mix well. Season.

4 Divide the cheese mixture between the baguettes, spread it over the cut surfaces and sandwich together. Wrap each baguette tightly in foil.

5 Heat the baguettes over the barbecue for about 10–15 minutes, turning them occasionally. Peel back the foil to check that they are cooked and the cheese mixture has melted. Serve with salad leaves (greens) and garnished with fresh herbs.

TIME SAVER

If there's no room on the barbecue, and you want to eat these at the same time as the rest of the food, bake them in a preheated oven at 200°C/400°F/Gas Mark 6 for 15 minutes.

CHEESEBURGERS IN BUNS WITH BARBECUE SAUCE

Soya mince and seasonings combine to make these tasty vegetarian burgers, which are topped with cheese, Tasty Barbecue Sauce, dill cucumber and tomato.

STEP 1

SERVES 4

150 g/ 5 oz/²/₃ cup dehydrated soya mince
300 ml/¹/₂ pint/ 1¹/₄ cups vegetable stock
1 small onion, chopped finely
125 g/4 oz/1 cup plain (all-purpose) flour
1 egg, beaten
1 tbsp chopped fresh herbs
1 tbsp mushroom ketchup or soy sauce
2 tbsp vegetable oil
4 burger buns
4 cheese slices
salt and pepper

TO GARNISH:
Tasty Barbecue Sauce (see page 14)
dill pickle
tomato slices

TO SERVE:
lettuce, cucumber & spring onion (scallion)
    salad

1 Put the soya mince into a large bowl. Pour over the vegetable stock and leave to soak for about 15 minutes until it has been absorbed.

2 Add the onion, flour, beaten egg and chopped herbs. Season with the mushroom ketchup or soy sauce and a little salt and pepper.

STEP 2

3 Form the mixture into 8 burgers. Cover and chill until ready to cook.

4 Brush the burgers with vegetable oil and barbecue them over hot coals, turning once. Allow about 5 minutes on each side.

5 Split the buns and top with a burger. Lay a cheese slice on top and garnish with barbecue sauce, dill pickle and tomato slices. Serve with a green salad made with lettuce, spring onion (scallion) and cucumber.

STEP 3

VARIATIONS

Flavour the burgers with different fresh herbs to vary the taste, or use mixed dried herbs for convenience.

Give the burgers a spicy flavour by adding ¹/₂–1 teaspoon of chilli powder to the mixture.

STEP 5

STEP 1

STEP 2

STEP 3

STEP 4

NAAN BREAD WITH CURRIED VEGETABLE KEBABS

Warmed Indian bread is served with barbecued vegetable kebabs, which are brushed with a curry-spiced yogurt baste.

SERVES 4

4 metal or wooden skewers (soak wooden skewers in warm water for 30 minutes)

YOGURT BASTE:
150 ml/¹/₄ pint/²/₃ cup natural yogurt
1 tbsp chopped fresh mint (or 1 tsp dried)
1 tsp ground cumin
1 tsp ground coriander
¹/₂ tsp chilli powder
pinch of turmeric
pinch of ground ginger
salt and pepper

KEBABS:
8 small new potatoes
1 small aubergine (eggplant)
1 courgette (zucchini), cut into chunks
8 chestnut (crimini) or closed-cup
mushrooms
8 small tomatoes
naan bread to serve
sprigs of fresh mint to garnish

1 To make the spiced yogurt baste, mix together the yogurt, mint, cumin, coriander, chilli powder, turmeric and ginger. Season with salt and pepper. Cover and chill.

2 Boil the potatoes until just tender. Meanwhile, chop the aubergine (eggplant) into chunks and sprinkle them liberally with salt. Leave for 10–15 minutes to extract the bitter juices. Rinse and drain them well. Drain the potatoes.

3 Thread the vegetables on to the skewers, alternating the different types.

4 Place them in a shallow dish and brush with the yogurt baste, coating them evenly. Cover and chill until ready to cook.

5 Wrap the naan bread in foil and place towards one side of the barbecue to warm through.

6 Cook the kebabs over the barbecue, basting with any remaining spiced yogurt, until they just begin to char slightly. Serve with the warmed Indian bread, garnished with sprigs of fresh mint.

STEP 1

STEP 2

STEP 3

STEP 4

MEDITERRANEAN STUFFED (BELL) PEPPERS

Halved (bell) peppers are stuffed with the flavours of the Mediterranean in this sunshine-bright dish.

SERVES 4

1 red (bell) pepper
1 green (bell) pepper
1 yellow (bell) pepper
1 orange (bell) pepper
6 tbsp olive oil
1 small red onion, sliced
1 small aubergine (eggplant), chopped
    roughly
125 g/4 oz button mushrooms, wiped
125 g/4 oz/1 cup cherry tomatoes, halved
few drops of mushroom ketchup
handful of fresh basil leaves, torn into pieces
2 tbsp lemon juice
salt and pepper
sprigs of fresh basil to garnish
lemon wedges to serve

1 Halve the (bell) peppers, remove the cores and deseed them. Sprinkle over a few drops of olive oil and season with a little salt and pepper.

2 Heat the remaining olive oil in a frying pan (skillet). Add the onion, aubergine (eggplant) and mushrooms, and fry for 3–4 minutes, stirring frequently. Remove from the heat and transfer to a mixing bowl.

3 Add the cherry tomatoes, mushroom ketchup, basil leaves and lemon juice to the aubergine (eggplant) mixture. Season well with salt and pepper.

4 Spoon the aubergine (eggplant) mixture into the (bell) pepper halves. Enclose in foil parcels (packages) and cook over the hot coals for about 15–20 minutes, turning once.

5 Unwrap carefully and serve garnished with sprigs of fresh basil. Serve with lemon wedges.

TIPS

These stuffed (bell) peppers can be made in advance and kept in the refrigerator, wrapped in foil, ready for cooking over the barbecue.

Dried herbs can be used instead of fresh ones if they are unavailable. Substitute 1 teaspoon of dried basil or use mixed dried Italian herbs as an alternative.

If you wish, top these stuffed (bell) peppers with grated Mozzarella or Cheddar cheese – 75 g/3 oz/^{1}/4 cup will be sufficient.

STEP 1

STEP 2

STEP 3

STEP 4

PITTA (POCKET) BREADS WITH GREEK SALAD & HOT ROSEMARY DRESSING

Pitta (pocket) breads are warmed over the hot coals, then split and filled with a Greek salad tossed in a fragrant rosemary dressing.

SERVES 4

½ iceberg lettuce, chopped roughly
2 large tomatoes, cut into wedges
7.5 cm/ 3 inch piece of cucumber, cut into chunks
30 g/ 1 oz/ ¼ cup pitted black olives
125 g/4 oz Feta cheese
4 pitta (pocket) breads

DRESSING:
6 tbsp olive oil
3 tbsp red wine vinegar
1 tbsp crushed fresh rosemary
½ tsp caster (superfine) sugar
salt and pepper

1 To make the salad, combine the lettuce, tomatoes, cucumber and olives.

2 Cut the Feta cheese into chunks and add to the salad. Toss gently.

3 To make the dressing, whisk together the olive oil, red wine vinegar, rosemary and sugar. Season to taste with salt and pepper. Place in a small saucepan or heatproof bowl and heat gently or place over the barbecue to warm through.

4 Wrap the pitta (pocket) breads tightly in foil and place over the hot barbecue for 2–3 minutes, turning once, to warm through.

5 Unwrap the breads and split them open. Fill with the salad mixture and drizzle over the warm dressing. Serve at once.

TIPS

Substitute different herbs for the rosemary – either oregano or basil would make a delicious alternative.

Pack plenty of the salad into the pitta (pocket) breads – they taste much better when packed full to bursting!

32

CHAPTER THREE

Main Courses

If you thought that vegetarian barbecues consisted of char-grilled mushroom kebabs, then these recipes will convince you to think again. True, mushrooms do make an appearance in a tempting recipe for brochettes, where they are combined with smoked tofu (bean curd) and basted with olive oil, lemon juice and garlic to make them taste really special. But how about Grilled Cypriot Cheese with Tomato, Red Onion & Coriander (Cilantro) Salad, Barbecued Bean Pot, or Vine (Grape) Leaf Parcels with Soft Cheese & Almonds? Throughout this chapter you will find appealing and imaginative recipes that will really spice up your barbecue!

Some preparation is needed before the barbecue starts, so that certain foods are soaking up their marinades, or are threaded on to skewers in readiness for cooking. The Barbecued Bean Pot needs to be pre-cooked in a conventional oven; the pot is then kept hot over the coals, ready for serving cowboy-style to your hungry guests.

All these recipes provide their fair share of protein – either from cheese, beans, chick-peas (garbanzo beans) or tofu (bean curd). And because they all contain vegetables of some description, they supply important vitamins, minerals and carbohydrates to the diet. Which all adds up to a bonus for food that tastes good too!

Opposite: *Use as wide a range of fresh vegetables as you can to create exotic and unusual dishes for your guests.*

STEP 1

STEP 2

STEP 3

STEP 4

MOZZARELLA WITH BARBECUED RADICCIO

Sliced Mozzarella cheese is served with sliced tomatoes and radiccio, which is singed over hot coals and drizzled with a basil, olive oil and pesto dressing.

SERVES 4

1 tbsp red or green pesto sauce
6 tbsp virgin olive oil
3 tbsp red wine vinegar
handful of fresh basil leaves
500 g/ 1 lb Mozzarella cheese
4 large tomatoes, sliced
2 radiccio
salt and pepper
fresh basil leaves to garnish

1 To make the dressing, mix the pesto sauce, olive oil and red wine vinegar together.

2 Tear the fresh basil leaves into tiny pieces and add them to the dressing. Season with a little salt and pepper.

3 Slice the Mozzarella cheese thinly and arrange it on 4 serving plates with the tomatoes.

4 Leaving the root end on the radiccio, slice each one into quarters. Barbecue them quickly, so that the leaves singe on the outside. Place two quarters on each serving plate.

5 Drizzle the dressing over the radiccio, cheese and tomatoes.

6 Garnish with extra basil leaves and serve immediately.

TIPS

When singeing the radiccio, it is a good idea to barbecue each quarter individually, holding it over the hot coals with tongs and turning it constantly.

If you can't find fresh basil, substitute oregano or marjoram instead. Tearing the basil leaves instead of chopping them helps to retain their peppery fragrance and flavour.

Pesto sauce is an aromatic olive oil, basil and pine kernel (nut) paste that can be bought in jars from supermarkets or delicatessens.

STEP 2

STEP 3

STEP 4

STEP 5

SMOKED TOFU (BEAN CURD) & MUSHROOM BROCHETTES

These tofu (bean curd) and mushroom kebabs are marinated in a lemon, garlic and herb mixture so that they soak up a delicious flavour.

SERVES 4

8 wooden skewers
1 lemon
1 garlic clove, crushed
4 tbsp olive oil
4 tbsp white wine vinegar
1 tbsp chopped fresh herbs, such as
  rosemary, parsley and thyme
300 g/10 oz smoked tofu (bean curd)
350 g/12 oz cup mushrooms, wiped
salt and pepper
fresh herbs to garnish

TO SERVE:
mixed salad leaves (greens)
cherry tomatoes, halved

1 Soak the wooden skewers in hand-hot water for 30 minutes.

2 Grate the rind from the lemon finely and squeeze out the juice.

3 Add the garlic, olive oil, vinegar and herbs to the lemon rind and juice, mixing well. Season to taste.

4 Slice the tofu (bean curd) into large chunks. Thread the pieces on to kebab sticks or wooden skewers, alternating them with the mushrooms.

5 Lay the kebabs in a shallow dish and pour over the marinade. Cover and chill for 1–2 hours, turning the kebabs in the marinade from time to time.

6 Cook the kebabs over the barbecue, brushing them with the marinade and turning often, for about 6 minutes.

7 Garnish with fresh herbs and serve with mixed salad leaves (greens) and cherry tomatoes.

EXTRA FLAVOUR

Firm tofu (bean curd) can be substituted for the smoked variety if you prefer.
  Thread small fresh bay leaves on to the skewers. They will help to give the kebabs a good flavour.

STEP 1

STEP 2

STEP 3

STEP 5

VINE (GRAPE) LEAF PARCELS WITH SOFT CHEESE & ALMONDS

A wonderful combination of cream cheese, chopped dates, ground almonds and lightly fried nuts is encased in vine (grape) leaves, which are wrapped in foil and cooked over the barbecue.

SERVES 4

300 g/10 oz/1¼ cups cream cheese
60 g/2 oz/¼ cup ground almonds
30 g/1 oz/2 tbsp dates, stoned (pitted) and
    chopped
30 g/1 oz/2 tbsp butter
30 g/1 oz/¼ cup flaked (slivered) almonds
12–16 vine (grape) leaves
salt and pepper

TO GARNISH:
sprigs of rosemary
tomato wedges

1 Beat the cream cheese in a large bowl to soften it.

2 Add the ground almonds and chopped dates, and mix together thoroughly. Season with salt and pepper.

3 Melt the butter in a small frying pan (skillet). Add the flaked (slivered) almonds and fry them gently for 2–3 minutes until golden brown. Remove from the heat and leave to cool for a few minutes.

4 Mix the fried nuts with the cream cheese mixture, stirring well to combine thoroughly.

5 Soak the vine (grape) leaves in water to remove some of the saltiness, if specified on the packet. Drain them, lay them out on a work surface (counter) and spoon an equal amount of the cream cheese mixture on to each one. Fold over the leaves to enclose the filling.

6 Wrap the vine (grape) leaf parcels in foil, 1 or 2 per foil package. Place over the barbecue to heat through for about 8–10 minutes, turning once.

7 Serve with barbecued baby corn and garnish with sprigs of rosemary and tomato wedges.

VARIATION

Omit the dates from the filling and substitute sultanas (golden raisins) or raisins. Ground and whole hazelnuts can be used instead of almonds.

TURKISH VEGETABLE KEBABS WITH SPICY CHICK-PEA (GARBANZO BEAN) SAUCE

A spicy chick-pea (garbanzo bean) sauce is served with barbecued vegetable kebabs.

SERVES 4

4 metal or wooden skewers (soak wooden skewers in warm water for 30 minutes)

SAUCE:
4 tbsp olive oil
3 garlic cloves, crushed
1 small onion, chopped finely
475 g/15 oz can of chick-peas (garbanzo beans), rinsed and drained
300 g/10 oz/1¼ cups natural yogurt
1 tsp cumin
½ tsp chilli powder
lemon juice
salt and pepper

KEBABS:
1 aubergine (eggplant)
1 red (bell) pepper, cored and deseeded
1 green (bell) pepper, cored and deseeded
4 plum tomatoes
1 lemon, cut into wedges
8 small fresh bay leaves
olive oil for brushing

1 To make the sauce, heat the olive oil in a small frying pan (skillet) and fry the garlic and onion gently until softened and golden brown, about 5 minutes.

2 Put the chick-peas (garbanzo beans) and yogurt into a blender or food processor and add the cumin, chilli powder and onion mixture. Blend for about 15 seconds until smooth. Alternatively, mash the chick-peas (garbanzo beans) and mix with the yogurt, cumin, chilli powder and onion.

3 Tip the puréed mixture into a bowl and season to taste with lemon juice, salt and pepper. Cover and chill until ready to serve.

4 To prepare the kebabs, cut the vegetables into large chunks and thread them on to the skewers, placing a bay leaf and lemon wedge at both ends of each kebab.

5 Brush the kebabs with olive oil and cook them over the barbecue, turning frequently, for about 5–8 minutes. Heat the chick-pea (garbanzo bean) sauce and serve with the kebabs.

> MILDER SAUCE
>
> To make a sauce with a milder flavour, substitute paprika for the chilli powder.

STEP 1

STEP 2

STEP 3

STEP 4

STEP 1

STEP 2

STEP 3

STEP 4

BARBECUED BEAN POT

Cook this tasty vegetable and Quorn casserole conventionally, then keep it piping hot over the barbecue. Its delicious aroma will cut through the fresh air to make appetites very keen! Soya cubes can be used in place of Quorn, if you prefer.

SERVES 4

60 g/2 oz/¼ cup butter or margarine
1 large onion, chopped
2 garlic cloves, crushed
2 carrots, sliced
2 celery sticks, sliced
1 tbsp paprika
2 tsp ground cumin
425 g/14 oz can of chopped tomatoes
475 g/15 oz can of mixed beans, rinsed and
    drained
150 ml/¼ pint/⅔ cup vegetable stock
1 tbsp molasses sugar or black treacle
    (molasses)
350 g/12 oz Quorn or soya cubes
salt and pepper

1 Melt the butter or margarine in a large flameproof casserole and fry the onion and garlic gently for about 5 minutes, until golden brown.

2 Add the carrots and celery, and cook for a further 2 minutes, then stir in the paprika and cumin.

3 Add the tomatoes and beans. Pour in the stock and add the sugar or treacle (molasses). Bring to the boil, then reduce the heat and simmer, uncovered, for 30 minutes, stirring occasionally.

4 Add the Quorn or soya cubes to the casserole and cook, covered, for a further 20 minutes. Stir the mixture occasionally.

5 Season to taste, then transfer the casserole to the barbecue, keeping it to one side to keep hot.

6 Ladle on to plates and serve with crusty French bread.

ALTERNATIVES

If you prefer, cook the casserole in a preheated oven at 190°C/375°F/Gas Mark 5 from step 3, but keep the dish covered.
  Instead of mixed beans you could use just one type of canned beans. Choose from red kidney beans, black eye beans (black-eyed peas), chick-peas (garbanzo beans) or soya beans.

STEP 2

STEP 3

STEP 4

STEP 6

GRILLED CYPRIOT CHEESE WITH TOMATO & RED ONION SALAD

Haloumi is a type of Cypriot cheese which remains firm and takes on a marvellous flavour when swiftly barbecued.

SERVES 4

500 g/1 lb Haloumi cheese
½ quantity Orange, Chive & Marjoram
  Marinade (see page 16)

SALAD:
250 g/8 oz plum tomatoes
1 small red onion
4 tbsp olive oil
2 tbsp cider vinegar
1 tsp lemon juice
pinch of ground coriander
2 tsp chopped fresh coriander (cilantro)
salt and pepper
fresh basil leaves to garnish

1 Slice the cheese quite thickly and place it in a shallow dish.

2 Pour the marinade over the cheese. Cover and chill for at least 30 minutes.

3 To make the salad, slice the tomatoes and arrange them on a serving plate. Slice the onion thinly and scatter over the tomatoes.

4 Whisk together the olive oil, vinegar, lemon juice, ground coriander and fresh coriander (cilantro).

5 Season to taste with salt and pepper, then drizzle the dressing over the tomatoes and onions. Cover and chill.

6 Drain the marinade from the Haloumi cheese. Cook the cheese over hot coals for 2 minutes, turning once. Lift on to plates and serve with the salad.

SERVING SUGGESTIONS

Warmed pitta (pocket) breads taste wonderful stuffed with the salad and topped with the barbecued Haloumi.

If Haloumi cheese is not available, you can use Feta cheese instead.

Serve the cheese and salad with crusty bread or potato salad to make it more filling.

CHAPTER FOUR

Salads

Lively salads are an essential accompaniment to barbecued food, supplying a pleasant change of taste and texture to refresh the palate. For something easy and quick to make, you could simply prepare a huge bowl of mixed salad leaves (greens), drizzled with one of the dressings from Chapter One, but here you will discover some new ideas for more unusual combinations.

These days it is so easy to make exciting salads with interesting ingredients. All year round supermarkets and shops are full of glorious vegetables and fruits from all over the world. We can make the most of seasonal, home-grown produce for flavour and economy, or we can buy imported foods for special occasions, or to perk up everyday ingredients to transform them into something special. We can certainly enjoy eating salads throughout the year, even if we can't always rely on the weather for a barbecue!

Any salad is only as good as the ingredients that you put into it, so be sure to choose produce from a reputable supplier, and use it when it is at its best. That way you will be making the most of its freshness and flavour, and you will be getting all the goodness that the fruit and vegetables contain.

Opposite: Fresh fruits and vegetables used in a range of imaginative salads will provide a refreshing accompaniment to the main course dishes.

STEP 1

STEP 2

STEP 3

STEP 4

CHAR-GRILLED VEGETABLES WITH SIDEKICK DRESSING

Colourful vegetables are barbecued over hot coals to make this unusual hot salad, which is served with a spicy chilli sauce on the side.

SERVES 4

1 red (bell) pepper, cored and deseeded
1 orange or yellow (bell) pepper, cored and
    deseeded
2 courgettes (zucchini)
2 corn-on-the-cob
1 aubergine (eggplant)
olive oil for brushing
chopped fresh thyme, rosemary and parsley
salt and pepper
lime or lemon wedges to serve

DRESSING:
2 tbsp olive oil
1 tbsp sesame oil
1 garlic clove, crushed
1 small onion, chopped finely
1 celery stick, chopped finely
1 small green chilli, deseeded and chopped
    finely
4 tomatoes, chopped
5 cm/2 inch piece cucumber, chopped finely
1 tbsp tomato purée (paste)
1 tbsp lime or lemon juice

1 To make the dressing, heat the olive and sesame oils together in a saucepan or frying pan (skillet). Add the garlic and onion, and fry together gently until softened, about 3 minutes.

2 Add the celery, chilli and tomatoes to the pan and cook, stirring occasionally, for 5 minutes over a medium heat.

3 Stir in the cucumber, tomato purée (paste) and lime or lemon juice, and simmer for 8–10 minutes until thick and pulpy. Season to taste with salt and pepper.

4 Cut the vegetables into thick slices and brush with a little olive oil.

5 Cook the vegetables over the hot coals for about 5-8 minutes, sprinkling them with salt and pepper and fresh herbs as they cook, and turning once.

6 Divide the vegetables between 4 serving plates and spoon some of the dressing on to the side. Serve at once, sprinkled with a few more chopped herbs and accompanied by the lime or lemon wedges.

STEP 1

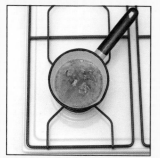

STEP 2

STEP 3

STEP 4

GOAT'S CHEESE WITH WALNUTS IN WARM OIL & VINEGAR DRESSING

This delicious salad combines soft goat's cheese with walnut halves. Served on a bed of mixed salad leaves (greens) and sprinkled with a warm walnut oil and wine vinegar dressing, it could double as a starter.

SERVES 4

90 g/ 3 oz/ 1 cup walnut halves
mixed salad leaves (greens)
125 g/ 4 oz soft goat's cheese
snipped fresh chives to garnish

DRESSING:
6 tbsp walnut oil
3 tbsp white wine vinegar
1 tbsp clear honey
1 tsp Dijon mustard
pinch of ground ginger
salt and pepper

1 To make the dressing, whisk together the walnut oil, wine vinegar, honey, mustard and ginger in a small saucepan. Season to taste.

2 Heat the dressing on the hob (stove top) or over the barbecue, stirring occasionally, until warm. Add the walnut halves to the warm dressing and continue to heat for 3–4 minutes.

3 Arrange the salad leaves on 4 serving plates and place spoonfuls of goat's cheese on top. Lift the walnut halves from the dressing with a perforated spoon, and scatter them over the salads.

4 Transfer the warm dressing to a small jug, for sprinkling over the salads.

5 Sprinkle chives over the salads and serve them, accompanied by the warm walnut oil dressing.

TIPS

Hazelnut oil makes a delicious alternative to walnut oil; if you use it, you can also replace the walnuts with hazelnuts if you wish.

If you are heating the dressing over the barbecue, choose an old saucepan, as it may become blackened on the outside.

CARROT & CASHEW NUT COLESLAW

This simple salad has a brilliant dressing made from poppy seeds pan-fried in sesame oil to bring out their flavour.

STEP 1

SERVES 4

1 large carrot, grated
1 small onion, chopped finely
2 celery sticks, chopped
¼ small, hard white cabbage, shredded
1 tbsp chopped fresh parsley
4 tbsp sesame oil
½ tsp poppy seeds
60 g/2 oz/½ cup cashew nuts
2 tbsp white wine or cider vinegar
salt and pepper
sprigs of fresh parsley to garnish

1 In a large salad bowl, mix together the carrot, onion, celery and cabbage. Stir in the chopped parsley.

2 Heat the sesame oil in a saucepan that has a lid. Add the poppy seeds and cover the pan. Cook over a medium high heat until the seeds start to make a popping sound. Remove from the heat and leave to cool.

3 Scatter the cashew nuts on to a baking sheet. Place them under a medium-hot grill (broiler) and toast until lightly browned, being careful not to burn them. Leave to cool.

4 Add the vinegar to the oil and poppy seeds, then pour over the carrot mixture. Add the cooled cashew nuts. Toss together to coat the salad ingredients with the dressing.

5 Garnish the salad with sprigs of parsley and serve.

STEP 2

STEP 3

VARIATIONS

Sesame seeds or sunflower seeds can be used in place of poppy seeds.

Substitute peanuts for cashew nuts if you prefer – they are more economical and taste every bit as good when lightly toasted.

STEP 4

STEP 1

STEP 2

STEP 3

STEP 4

HONEYDEW & STRAWBERRY SALAD WITH COOL CUCUMBER DRESSING

This refreshing fruit-based salad is perfect for a hot summer's day.

SERVES 4

½ iceberg lettuce, shredded
1 small honeydew melon
250 g/8 oz/1½ cups strawberries, hulled
  and sliced
5 cm/2 inch piece of cucumber, sliced thinly
sprigs of fresh mint to garnish

DRESSING:
200 g/7 oz/scant 1 cup natural yogurt
5 cm/2 inch piece of cucumber, peeled
a few fresh mint leaves
½ tsp finely grated lime or lemon rind
pinch of caster (superfine) sugar
3–4 ice cubes

1 Arrange the shredded lettuce on 4
serving plates.

2 Cut the melon lengthways into
quarters. Scoop out the seeds and
cut through the flesh down to the skin at
2.5 cm/1 inch intervals. Cut the melon
close to the skin and detach the flesh.

3 Place the chunks of melon on the
bed of lettuce with the strawberries
and cucumber.

4 To make the dressing, put the
yogurt, cucumber, mint leaves,
lime or lemon rind, caster (superfine)
sugar and ice cubes into a blender or food
processor. Blend together for about 15
seconds until smooth. Alternatively,
chop the cucumber and mint finely,
crush the ice cubes and combine with the
other ingredients.

5 Serve the salad with a little dressing
poured over it. Garnish with sprigs
of fresh mint.

VARIATIONS

Omit the ice cubes in the dressing if you
prefer, but make sure that the ingredients
are well-chilled. This will ensure that the
finished dressing is really cool.

   Charentais, cantaloup or ogen melon
can be substituted for honeydew.

THREE-WAY POTATO SALAD

There's nothing to beat the flavour of new potatoes, served just warm in a delicious dressing.

STEP 1

STEP 2

STEP 3

STEP 4

EACH DRESSING SERVES **4**

LIGHT CURRY DRESSING:
1 tbsp vegetable oil
1 tbsp medium curry paste
1 small onion, chopped
1 tbsp mango chutney, chopped
6 tbsp natural yogurt
3 tbsp single (light) cream
2 tbsp mayonnaise
salt and pepper
1 tbsp single (light) cream to garnish

WARM VINAIGRETTE DRESSING:
6 tbsp hazelnut oil
3 tbsp cider vinegar
1 tsp wholegrain mustard
1 tsp caster (superfine) sugar
few basil leaves, torn into shreds
salt and pepper

PARSLEY, SPRING ONION (SCALLION)
& SOURED CREAM DRESSING:
150 ml/$^1/_4$ pint/$^2/_3$ cup soured cream
3 tbsp light mayonnaise
4 spring onions (scallions), trimmed and
*   chopped finely*
1 tbsp chopped fresh parsley
salt and pepper

500 g/1lb new potatoes for each dressing
fresh herbs to garnish

1 To make the Light Curry Dressing, heat the vegetable oil in a saucepan and add the curry paste and onion. Fry together, stirring frequently, until the onion is soft, about 5 minutes. Remove from the heat and leave to cool slightly.

2 Mix together the mango chutney, yogurt, cream and mayonnaise. Add the curry mixture and blend together. Season with salt and pepper.

3 To make the Vinaigrette Dressing, whisk the hazelnut oil, cider vinegar, mustard, sugar and basil together in a small jug or bowl. Season with salt and pepper.

4 To make the Parsley, Spring Onion (Scallion) & Soured Cream Dressing, mix all the ingredients together until thoroughly combined. Season with salt and pepper.

5 Cook the potatoes in lightly salted boiling water until just tender. Drain well and leave to cool for 5 minutes, then add the chosen dressing, tossing to coat. Serve, garnished with fresh herbs, spooning a little single (light) cream on to the potatoes if you have used the curry dressing.

STEP 2

STEP 3

STEP 4

STEP 5

DEEP SOUTH SPICED RICE & BEANS

Cajun spices add a flavour of the American deep south to this colourful rice and red kidney bean salad.

SERVES 4

175 g/6 oz/scant 1 cup long-grain rice
4 tbsp olive oil
1 small green (bell) pepper, cored, deseeded and chopped
1 small red (bell) pepper, cored, deseeded and chopped
1 onion, chopped finely
1 small red or green chilli, deseeded and chopped finely
2 tomatoes, chopped
125 g/4 oz/¹/₂ cup canned red kidney beans, rinsed and drained
1 tbsp chopped fresh basil
2 tsp chopped fresh thyme (or 1 tsp dried)
1 tsp Cajun spice
salt and pepper
fresh basil leaves to garnish

1 Cook the rice in plenty of boiling, lightly salted water until just tender, about 12 minutes. Rinse with cold water and drain well.

2 Meanwhile, heat the olive oil in a frying pan (skillet) and fry the green and red (bell) peppers and onion together gently until softened, about 5 minutes.

3 Add the chilli and tomatoes, and cook for a further 2 minutes.

4 Add the vegetable mixture and red kidney beans to the rice. Stir well to combine thoroughly.

5 Stir the chopped herbs and Cajun spice into the rice mixture. Season well with salt and pepper, and serve, garnished with basil leaves.

CHILLIES

The fresh red or green chilli can be replaced by 1 tsp chilli powder, for speed and convenience.

Take care when handling fresh chillies, as the residue from them can burn or irritate the skin. Be especially careful to avoid rubbing your eyes when preparing them, and rinse your hands well after handling them.

CHAPTER FIVE

Desserts

By the time everyone at the barbecue has eaten their fill of main course foods, there is hardly any room left for dessert. But for those who are confirmed pudding-lovers, a meal would not seem complete without something to finish off with. The recipes in this chapter offer the ideal solution.

The dishes that follow in the next few pages are light, yet full of flavour. There are three recipes to cook over the coals, a couple of fresh fruit salad combinations and an easy recipe for Giggle Cake that will keep the children happy. They will also love the Banana & Marshmallow Melts that are served oozing with butterscotch sauce, and there is even a recipe for addicted chocoholics – a fabulous Hot Chocolate Dip that is served with tropical fruit kebabs. Remember to keep a jug of cream at the ready, and some ice cream in the freezer, just for those who can't resist an extra helping of indulgence.

Make two or three of the recipes here if you are planning to make a real day of your barbecue party. And don't forget, people often wander back for seconds even if they thought they were full up half an hour before. So make plenty, as all of these desserts are worth making room for!

Opposite: *Fresh fruits from home and abroad provide a delicious basis for some barbecued desserts.*

STEP 2

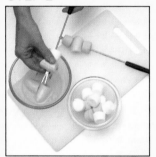

STEP 3

STEP 4

STEP 5

BANANA & MARSHMALLOW MELTS WITH BUTTERSCOTCH SAUCE

This simply delicious dessert will go down a treat with children of all ages. Bananas and marshmallows taste fantastic with the warm butterscotch sauce.

SERVES 4

4 wooden skewers
4 bananas
4 tbsp lemon juice
250 g/8 oz pkt marshmallows

SAUCE:
125 g/4 oz/¹/₂ cup butter
125 g/4 oz/²/₃ cup light muscovado sugar
125 g/4 oz/¹/₃ cup golden (light corn) syrup
4 tbsp hot water

1 Soak the wooden skewers in hand-hot water for 30 minutes.

2 Slice the bananas into large chunks and dip them into the lemon juice to prevent them from going brown.

3 Thread the marshmallows and pieces of banana alternately on to kebab sticks or bamboo skewers, placing 2 marshmallows and 1 piece of banana on to each one.

4 To make the sauce, melt the butter, sugar and syrup together in a small saucepan. Add the hot water, stirring until blended and smooth. Do not boil or else the mixture will become toffee-like.

Keep the sauce warm at the edge of the barbecue, stirring from time to time.

5 Sear the kebabs over the barbecue coals for 30–40 seconds, turning constantly, so that the marshmallows just begin to brown and melt.

6 Serve the kebabs with some of the butterscotch sauce spooned over.

SERVING SUGGESTIONS

The warm butterscotch sauce tastes wonderful with vanilla ice cream. Make double the quantity of sauce if you plan to serve ice cream at the barbecue.

Ideally, prepare the kebabs just before they are cooked to prevent the bananas from turning brown. The sauce can be prepared in advance, though.

You can heat whole bananas in their skins over the barbecue. When blackened, split the skins open and serve the bananas in their skins with a spoonful of the sauce.

STEP 1

STEP 2

STEP 3

STEP 4

CHAR-COOKED PINEAPPLE WITH GINGER & BROWN SUGAR BUTTER

Fresh pineapple slices are cooked on the barbecue, and brushed with a buttery fresh ginger and brown sugar baste.

SERVES 4

1 fresh pineapple

BUTTER:
125 g/4 oz/¹/₂ cup butter
90 g/3 oz/¹/₂ cup light muscovado sugar
1 tsp finely grated fresh root ginger

TOPPING:
250 g/8 oz/1 cup natural fromage frais
¹/₂ tsp ground cinnamon
1 tbsp light muscovado sugar

1 Prepare the fresh pineapple by cutting off the spiky top. Peel the pineapple with a sharp knife and cut into thick slices.

2 To make the ginger-flavoured butter, put the butter, sugar and ginger into a small saucepan and heat gently until melted. Transfer to a heatproof bowl and keep warm at the side of the barbecue, ready for basting the fruit.

3 To prepare the topping, mix together the fromage frais, cinnamon and sugar. Cover and chill until ready to serve.

4 Barbecue the pineapple slices for about 2 minutes on each side, brushing them with the ginger butter baste.

5 Serve the pineapple with a little extra ginger butter sauce poured over. Top with a spoonful of the spiced fromage frais.

VARIATIONS

If you prefer, substitute ¹/₂ teaspoon ground ginger for the grated fresh root ginger.

Light muscovado sugar gives the best flavour, but you can use ordinary soft brown sugar instead.

You can make this dessert indoors by cooking the pineapple under a hot grill (broiler), basting it as above with the melted ginger butter.

STEP 2

STEP 3

STEP 3

STEP 4

TOASTED TROPICAL FRUIT KEBABS WITH HOT CHOCOLATE DIP

Spear some chunks of exotic tropical fruits on to kebab sticks, sear them over the barbecue and serve with this amazing chocolate dip.

SERVES 4

4 wooden skewers

DIP:
125 g/4 oz/4 squares plain (dark)
*   chocolate, broken into pieces*
2 tbsp golden (light corn) syrup
1 tbsp cocoa powder
1 tbsp cornflour (cornstarch)
200 ml/7 fl oz /generous ³/₄ cup milk

KEBABS:
1 mango
1 paw-paw (papaya)
2 kiwi fruit
¹/₂ small pineapple
1 large banana
2 tbsp lemon juice
150 ml/¹/₄ pint/²/₃ cup white rum

1 Soak the wooden skewers in hand-hot water for 30 minutes.

2 Put all the ingredients for the chocolate dip into a saucepan. Heat, stirring constantly, until thickened and smooth. Keep warm at the edge of the barbecue.

3 Slice the mango on each side of its large, flat stone (pit). Cut the flesh into chunks, removing the peel. Halve, deseed and peel the paw-paw (papaya) and cut it into chunks. Peel the kiwi fruit and slice into chunks. Peel and cut the pineapple into chunks. Peel and slice the banana and dip the pieces in the lemon juice.

4 Thread the pieces of fruit alternately on to the wooden skewers. Place them in a shallow dish and pour over the rum. Leave to soak up the flavour of the rum until ready to barbecue, at least 30 minutes.

5 Cook the kebabs over the hot coals, turning frequently, until seared, about 2 minutes. Serve, accompanied by the hot chocolate dip.

VARIATIONS

Milk chocolate can be used in the chocolate dip instead of plain (dark), and honey could be substituted for golden (light corn) syrup.

For the kebabs, use any fruit you like, providing it can be threaded on to skewers. Peaches, nectarines, apples and grapes are all suitable.

GIGGLE CAKE

It's a mystery how this cake got its name – perhaps it's because it's easy to make and fun to eat. It takes only minutes to put together.

STEP 1

SERVES 8

350 g/12 oz/2 cups mixed dried fruit
125 g/4 oz/¹/₂ cup butter or margarine
175 g/6 oz/1 cup soft brown sugar
250 g/8 oz/2 cups self-raising flour
pinch of salt
2 eggs, beaten
225 g/7¹/₂ oz can of chopped pineapple,
* drained*
125 g/4 oz/¹/₂ cup glacé (candied) cherries,
* halved*

1 Put the mixed dried fruit into a large bowl and cover with boiling water. Leave to soak for 10–15 minutes, then drain well.

2 Put the butter or margarine and sugar into a large saucepan and heat gently until melted. Add the drained mixed dried fruit and cook over a low heat, stirring frequently, for 4–5 minutes. Remove from the heat and transfer to a mixing bowl. Leave to cool.

3 Sift the flour and salt into the dried fruit mixture and stir well. Add the eggs, mixing until thoroughly incorporated.

4 Add the pineapples and cherries to the cake mixture and stir to combine. Transfer to a greased and lined 1 kg/2 lb loaf tin (pan) and level the surface.

5 Bake in a preheated oven at 180°C/350°F/Gas Mark 4 for about 1 hour. Test the cake with a fine skewer; if it comes out clean, the cake is cooked. If not, return to the oven for a few more minutes.

STEP 2

STEP 3

VARIATIONS

If you wish, add 1 teaspoon ground mixed (apple pie) spice to the cake mixture, sifting it in with the flour.

Bake the cake in an 18 cm/7 inch round cake tin (pan) if you don't have a loaf tin (pan) of the right size. Remember to grease and line it first.

STEP 4

STEP 1

STEP 2

STEP 3

STEP 5

GREEN FRUIT SALAD WITH MINT & LEMON SYRUP

This delightful fresh fruit salad is the perfect finale for a summer barbecue. It has a lovely light syrup made with fresh mint and honey.

SERVES 4

1 small Charentais or honeydew melon
2 green apples
125 g/4 oz/1 cup seedless white (green) grapes
2 kiwi fruit
sprigs of fresh mint to decorate

SYRUP:
1 lemon
150 ml/¹/₄ pint/²/₃ cup white wine
150 ml/¹/₄ pint/²/₃ cup water
4 tbsp clear honey
few sprigs of fresh mint

1 To make the syrup, pare the rind from the lemon using a potato peeler.

2 Put the lemon rind into a saucepan with the wine, water and honey. Heat and simmer gently for 10 minutes. Remove from the heat. Add the sprigs of mint and leave to cool.

3 Slice the melon in half and scoop out the seeds. Use a melon baller or a teaspoon to make melon balls.

4 Core and chop the apples. Peel and slice the kiwi fruit.

5 Strain the cooled syrup into a serving bowl, removing and reserving the lemon rind and discarding the mint sprigs. Add the apple, grapes, kiwi and melon. Stir through gently to mix.

6 Serve, decorated with sprigs of fresh mint and some of the reserved lemon rind.

SERVING SUGGESTION

Serve the fruit salad in an attractive glass dish. Chill the dish for 20 minutes first, then keep the fruit salad cold by placing the dish in a large bowl of crushed ice or ice cubes.

STEP 1

STEP 2

STEP 3

STEP 4

BLACKBERRY, APPLE & FRESH FIG COMPOTE WITH HONEY YOGURT

Elderflower cordial is used in the syrup for this refreshing fruit compôte, giving it a delightfully summery flavour.

SERVES 4

1 lemon
60 g/ 2 oz/¼ cup caster (superfine) sugar
4 tbsp elderflower cordial
300 ml/½ pint/ 1¼ cups water
4 dessert (eating) apples
250 g/ 8 oz/ 2 cups blackberries
2 fresh figs

TOPPING:
150 g/ 5 oz/⅔ cup thick, creamy natural
   yogurt
2 tbsp clear honey

1 Pare the rind from the lemon using a potato peeler. Squeeze the juice. Put the lemon rind and juice into a saucepan with the sugar, elderflower cordial and water. Heat gently and simmer, uncovered, for 10 minutes.

2 Peel, core and slice the apples, and add them to the saucepan. Simmer gently for about 4–5 minutes until just tender. Leave to cool.

3 Transfer the apples and syrup to a serving bowl and add the blackberries. Slice and add the figs. Stir gently to mix. Cover and chill until ready to serve.

4 Spoon the yogurt into a small serving bowl and drizzle the honey over the top. Cover and chill, then serve with the fruit salad.

ELDERFLOWERS AND CREAM

Elderflower cordial is easy to obtain from supermarkets, health-food shops and delicatessens. Alternatively, you can use a blackberry or apple cordial instead. Do not prepare the apples until the syrup is ready, or they will begin to turn brown.

Fresh whipped cream is delicious served with this fruit salad. If you are choosing cream for whipping, buy either double (heavy) cream or whipping cream. Double cream labelled as 'extra thick' is only suitable for spooning, and will not whip.

USING A BARBECUE

TIPS FOR BARBECUING FOOD

First and foremost, treat food for barbecuing with care – it should be kept chilled in the refrigerator or in a cool box, complete with ice packs, until ready to cook.

Light the barbecue in plenty of time, remembering that you will need about 45 minutes for charcoal to heat and about 10–15 minutes for a gas barbecue to become hot enough.

Food cooks best over glowing embers, not smoking fuel, so avoid putting the food over the hot coals until the smoking has subsided.

Oil the barbecue rack lightly before adding the food, to help to prevent it from sticking, and oil the skewers, tongs and barbecue fork for the same reason.

Control the heat by adjusting the distance of the food from the coals, or by altering the controls on a gas barbecue. Ideally, food should not be cooked too quickly, or else it will blacken and char on the outside before the middle is cooked – it needs time for the distinctive barbecued taste to be imparted.

VEGETABLES

For kebabs, choose a mixture of vegetables that will all cook at the same rate, and cut the chunks into roughly the same size. Choose from aubergines (eggplants), tomatoes, sliced corn-on-the-cob or baby corn,

The recipes in *Vegetarian Barbecues* are a welcome alternative to all those summertime meat-eaters' feasts. This book offers simple, delicious barbecue dishes for people who are committed vegetarians, for those who cook for them, or just for anyone who enjoys eating tasty vegetarian food!

The very idea of vegetarian barbecues seems odd to many people, who would probably only be able to think of cooking vegetable kebabs or stuffed jacket potatoes. Yet there are so many tasty and nutritious vegetarian recipes that can be cooked over hot coals – after all, barbecuing is just an alternative method of cooking by direct heat. Like grilling (broiling) and roasting, barbecuing cooks food quickly, so it can be applied successfully to all sorts of vegetarian dishes, as this book goes to show.

There is certainly something special about food cooked outdoors – it always tastes so good! It is almost as if the fresh air itself permeates the food and contributes to its flavour. Or perhaps it is just that we enjoy the sunshine and relaxation that is all part of the barbecue scenario. Whatever the reason, there is no doubt that the aromas and flavours of barbecued food are truly wonderful. So make the most of the summer months by doing your cooking and entertaining outside. The recipes in this book have all been devised with speed, convenience and appetizing food in mind, so that cooking is less of a chore, and more like good fun!

CHOOSING YOUR BARBECUE

These days, there are many different types of barbecue available, and your choice really depends on whether you think you will be going into barbecuing in a big way, or whether it will just be an occasional outdoor venture. The space available in your garden or on your patio will influence the size and type of equipment you choose – there's not much point in having a huge brick-built barbecue if your back garden is the size of a postage stamp! Likewise, if you are only catering for small numbers, you may not need anything too grand.

Get a feel for what is available by having a good look around garden centres, DIY shops, supermarkets, cook shops, department stores and hardware merchants. Before you buy, ask yourself a few questions about your needs – think about where you will use your barbecue and how often. Consider whether you want a portable type that can easily be lifted from one part of your garden to another. Will you be able to store the barbecue in winter and if so, does it dismantle easily? How big a barbecue do you need – are you cooking for crowds or just a cosy twosome? And is the barbecue the correct height? It could be very uncomfortable cooking on it if it is too low for you.

Whatever your constraints and considerations, it is always worthwhile buying the best quality barbecue within your price range to give you good service. And for safety reasons, make sure that you buy one that is stable and sturdy, as it could be very dangerous if not.

TYPES OF BARBECUE

Brick-built barbecues

For serious barbecuing, a brick-built construction is ideal, providing that you have the room for a permanent fixture. Make sure that you position it wisely – not too close to trees or the garden shed! The bricks do not have to be cemented together – if you prefer, they can be stacked so that the barbecue can be dismantled easily.

Self-assembly kits can be bought, which include a cooking grid, a charcoal grid and a metal base. They usually also contain pegs which are embedded into the wall of the barbecue to provide different levels for cooking the food. You will have to buy the bricks separately, which could be costly as you may need about a hundred.

Wagon barbecues

These barbecues are usually quite large, and can be moved around on wheels – a good idea if you want to position your barbecue near the house one day and in the evening sun the next, or move it from one end of the patio to the other. They may have hooks for hanging utensils, and shelves for barbecue equipment or for storing the charcoal.

The principle for barbecuing remains the same: the barbecue has a large rectangular area for the charcoal, above which is the grid to support the food. Check the storage possibilities for these types – some feature a removable fire box, which enables the wagon to be folded flat. This is invaluable if you don't have a garage or shed in which to store your barbecue over the winter months, as a barbecue can be a cumbersome and messy thing to store.

Freestanding barbecues

These are a very popular choice for people with small gardens and patios, and for those who just use them occasionally. They are supported on legs, bringing them to a sensible working height. They can be round or rectangular, and they vary in their degree of sophistication – some have variable heights for the cooking grid, shelves, a wind shield, a warming rack or serving shelf and a rod for spit-roasting food. Choose the right size, shape and quality for your needs at a price that is within your budget.

Portable barbecues

These are particularly suitable for cooking food for a small number of people, and are ideal for setting on to a firm base or table top to work from. It is usually possible to move the food closer to the heat by means of notches set at varying heights above the coals into which the grid can be slotted. Fold-up versions are often available.

Disposable barbecues

Ideal for picnics, beach barbecues or camping, these are designed to be used only once. Small and cheap to buy, they consist of a foil tray with specially impregnated coals. A grid supports the mushrooms and courgettes (zucchini).

New potatoes, onions, carrots, parsnips and Jerusalem artichokes can also be barbecued, but will need a little pre-cooking first.

If you are going to serve jacket potatoes, cook them first too – either conventionally or in a microwave oven for speed. Wrap in foil and keep warm to one side of the barbecue, ready for filling with one of the delicious ideas suggested on page 22. Alternatively, you can finish cooking potatoes directly on the grid over the coals, barbecuing them until the skins are crisp and brown.

Vegetables can be cooked in foil parcels as well as on kebab skewers. Slice them roughly, sprinkle with olive oil, herbs and seasonings and wrap tightly. Cook over the barbecue until tender – test with a skewer to check whether they are done.

HERBS

Have some fresh herbs to hand for throwing on to the coals. They smell wonderful as they burn, and will add extra flavour to your food. Woody herbs such as rosemary, thyme and bay leaves burn slowly, so they are good choices.

SALADS AND SIDE DISHES

Keep salads and other accompaniments fresh and chilled in the refrigerator, or in a cool box with ice packs. Ask for some help in carrying them outside when the barbecued food is almost cooked. Have plates, cutlery and serving spoons at the ready, so that there is no need to keep dashing indoors. And don't forget the salt and pepper!

DESSERTS

It is a good idea to serve a selection of desserts at barbecues – nothing too fancy or complicated is needed, just something to refresh the palate or provide a change of taste. Fresh fruit salads are always a good choice, and a couple of different types of fruit kebab will go down well, particularly if served with a delicious sauce. See the Desserts chapter for some mouthwatering suggestions.

COOKING TIME

Cooking times for barbecuing are difficult to give exactly, as it will depend on how fierce the heat is, the distance of the food from the coals and the type of food being cooked. Test the food from time to time to check whether it is done to your liking.

food as it cooks, and there is sufficient fuel to last for about an hour.

Gas barbecues

Charcoal is abandoned in this type of barbecue, and gas – usually butane – is used to heat lava rocks instead. These models are quick and convenient to use, as you don't have to light the coals and wait for the same length of time before the barbecue is ready. The special rocks heat through in about 15 minutes.

Another advantage of lava rocks is that they can be used over and over again, although they will need replacing occasionally – you will know when to do this, as the rocks will begin to flare up frequently during cooking. The food cooks in the same way over the 'coals' and achieves the same delicious taste, as the hot oil or liquid from the food drips down on to the rocks and creates the smoke that gives the food its distinctive barbecued flavour.

Portable gas barbecues and larger, more sophisticated wagon-types often have adjustable heat settings. These are especially suitable for bigger events and for families who hold barbecues regularly throughout the summer months, as they are ready quickly, and can be kept burning for a long time more easily than charcoal barbecues.

BARBECUE FUEL

Charcoal is used to fuel most barbecues, with the exception of gas-fired types, which heat lava rocks instead. Charcoal is available as briquettes, which burn the longest, or lumpwood, which is easier to ignite. It is also possible to buy 'barbecue

fuel' which is a charcoal substitute, although you may find that this does not burn quite so well.

Always remember to store charcoal and barbecue fuel in a dry place – if it is allowed to get damp, it may take you a long time to ignite it.

SAFETY TIPS

Choose a safe place for setting up your barbecue. It must be on a level surface, away from trees, bushes, fences and sheds. Try to position the barbecue well away from children's play areas and avoid setting it up in a place where your guests would hamper your activities.

Take great care when lighting a barbecue – and *never* use petrol, paraffin or methylated spirits. You can buy special gels and liquids for lighting barbecues, but always read the instructions on the pack first. You may need some extra-long matches or tapers to help you to ignite the barbecue.

Keep children well away from the barbecue – they don't always realize how hot it is. If they want to help, offer them a job threading food on to kebab skewers (if they are old enough to cope with this safely) or bringing things out from the kitchen.

Have a bucket of sand ready to throw over the barbecue in case there are any mishaps and it catches fire – soil makes a good alternative. Neither improve the taste of the food, so take care that it doesn't happen!

ACCESSORIES

Make sure that you are well-equipped with utensils that will make the cook's life easier when standing at the barbecue. A set of long tongs, a barbecue fork, plenty of long skewers and a fish slice (spatula) for serving the food will all come in handy. Long-handled brushes for basting the food with marinades and sauces will also be required. A couple of old saucepans are very useful for heating sauces and keeping them warm on the metal grill.

Some barbecues have rôtisserie attachments, which are ideal for cooking large joints of meat. These are only suitable if you have plenty of room on your barbecue, but are excellent for ensuring the meat is evenly cooked.

For safety, have a thick pair of oven gloves at the ready for picking up hot skewers or hot handles. Protect your clothes too, and wear a great big apron! Plastic aprons are good, as they wipe clean easily.

PLANNING YOUR BARBECUE

Timing

Make your life easier by preparing lots of tasty food that doesn't take for ever to cook – check the ideas in this book for inspiration. Whenever food is being barbecued, there always seems to be a long wait – even though it may only be minutes – so have a few dips and nibbles for your hungry guests. These can all be made in advance and kept chilled until needed. Raw vegetable crudités can be chopped and prepared beforehand too – just keep them chilled in sealed polythene bags until ready to serve.

Barbecues always take longer to get going than you expect, so allow plenty of time. Don't be tempted to start cooking too soon, or the coals will not be ready. The flames should have died down and the coals reduced to a steady glow before you begin.

Don't attempt to cook for a large party on a small barbecue, as it could take hours to feed everyone! In this situation, it is better to cook most of the food in the kitchen, and provide only a few barbecued items. Vegetarian sausages and burgers are ideal, as they cook quickly and can be barbecued in large quantities even on a small barbecue.

Planning ahead

Many foods for barbecuing will benefit from being marinated, especially dishes using tofu (bean curd) or Quorn (mycoprotein), which will absorb the flavour of the marinade – the longer they can be left to soak up the flavours, the better they will taste. You can buy tofu (bean curd) in four varieties – smoked, firm, soft or silken; use smoked or firm for kebabs, soft for adding to burgers and silken for adding to sauces and dips.

Have your kebabs ready-threaded for quick cooking; if possible, choose flat metal skewers so that the food does not slide as the kebabs are turned. Alternatively, use bamboo sticks – but remember to soak these in water beforehand so that they do not burn over the hot coals.

Make sweet and savoury sauces in advance if you can – the barbecue sauce, the butterscotch sauce for the Banana & Marshmallow Melts and the Hot Chocolate Dip for the Tropical Fruit Kebabs can all be prepared ahead of time.

CLEANING UP!

When you have enjoyed the barbecue and all the food is finished, you only have the clearing up left to do! The best idea is to delegate – after all, you've already done the preparation, so let someone else do the cleaning jobs.

Your barbecue equipment will appreciate being looked after, and it will last longer too, so do take care of it. Before attempting to clean it, allow the embers to become completely cold.

Empty the ashes and use a wire brush to clean the barbecue rack. If necessary, use one of the proprietary barbecue cleaning products to remove any stubborn stains.

Pack the barbecue away if it is portable, or dismantle it and store it in a dry place at the end of the season, ready for its reappearance next summer.

It is always worth buying fresh charcoal or fuel after a barbecue, to be sure of having enough the next time. This way an impromptu barbecue is not spoiled by not being able to get hold of a bag of charcoal at just the right moment. Store the fuel in a warm, dry place away from any heat source or naked flames. Keep well out of the reach of children, and make sure also that lighter fluids and cleaning fluids are securely capped and stored out of reach.

INDEX

LIVING IN THE WILD: PRIMATES

BONOBOS

Buffy Silverman

www.raintreepublishers.co.uk
Visit our website to find out
more information about
Raintree books.

To order:
☎ Phone 0845 6044371
▯ Fax +44 (0) 1865 312263
▯ Email myorders@raintreepublishers.co.uk

Customers from outside the UK please telephone +44 1865 312262

Raintree is an imprint of Capstone Global Library
Limited, a company incorporated in England and
Wales having its registered office at 7 Pilgrim Street,
London, EC4V 6LB – Registered company number:
6695582

Text © Capstone Global Library Limited 2012
First published in hardback in 2012
The moral rights of the proprietor have been asserted.

Edited by Abby Colich, Jilly Hunt, and Vaarunika
  Dharmapala
Designed by Victoria Allen
Picture research by Tracy Cummins
Original illustrations © Capstone Global Library
  Ltd 2012
Illustrations by Oxford Designers & Illustrators and
  HL Studios
Originated by Capstone Global Library Ltd
Printed and bound in China by CTPS

ISBN 978 1 406 23301 8 (hardback)
16 15 14 13 12
10 9 8 7 6 5 4 3 2 1

British Library Cataloguing in Publication Data
Silverman, Buffy.
Bonobos. -- (Living in the wild. Primates)
599.8'85-dc22
A full catalogue record for this book is available from
the British Library.

Acknowledgements
We would like to thank the following for permission
to reproduce photographs: Alamy pp. 14 (© A&J
Visage), 35 (© Photoshot Holdings Ltd); Corbis
pp. 38 (© Goran Tomasevic/Reuters), 39 (© Ian
Nichols/National Geographic), 41 (© Dominique
Derda/France 2); FLPA pp. 5 (Cyril Ruoso/Minden
Pictures), 20 (Cyril Ruoso), 26 (Frans Lanting),
30 (Frans Lanting), 31 (Cyril Ruoso), 44 (Frans
Lanting); Getty Images pp. 36 (Brent Stirton),
37 (Eric Feferberg); istockphoto p. 7
(© Michael Price); National Geographic pp. 8
(Frans Lanting), 15 (Cyril Ruoso/JH Editorial/
Minden Pictures), 22 (Cyril Ruoso/Minden Pictures);
National Geographic Stock p. 43 (Frans Lanting);
Photolibrary pp. 13 (Cyril Ruoso), 17 (Cyril Ruoso),
18 (Cyril Ruoso), 25 (Renaud Fulconis), 29
(Renaud Fulconis), 33 (Cyril Ruoso/Minden
Pictures); Photoshot pp. 19 (NPHA), 23 (NPHA);
Shutterstock pp. 6 (© worldswildlifewonders),
9 (© Kristof Degreef), 24 (© Uryadnikov Sergey).

Cover photograph of a young bonobo at Lola
Ya Bonobo Sanctuary, DRC, reproduced with
permission of Photolibrary (Renaud Fulconis).

Every effort has been made to contact copyright
holders of any material reproduced in this book.
Any omissions will be rectified in subsequent
printings if notice is given to the publisher.

Contents

Some words are shown in bold, **like this**. You can find out what they mean by looking in the glossary.

What are primates?

High-pitched screeches fill the forest. A group of bonobos chatter as they gather fruit from the trees. While some of them eat, others extend their hands to beg for food. The bonobos share their meal.

Bonobos are primates. Primates are a group of **mammals** which includes monkeys, apes, and humans. Lemurs, lorises, bushbabies, and tarsiers are primates, too. There are more than 350 different kinds of primates.

This map shows where in the world non-human primates live.

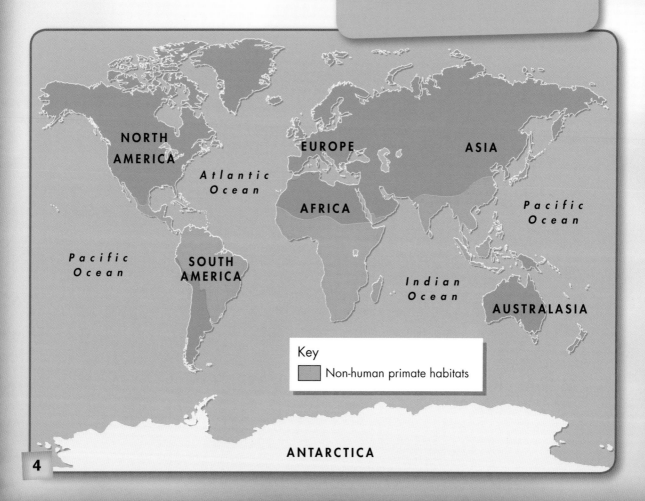

NORTH AMERICA

EUROPE

ASIA

Atlantic Ocean

AFRICA

Pacific Ocean

Pacific Ocean

SOUTH AMERICA

Indian Ocean

AUSTRALASIA

Key

Non-human primate habitats

ANTARCTICA

Like all mammals, primates have fur and produce milk for their babies to drink. They give birth to live babies and care for their young. They breathe air and keep a constant, warm body temperature.

Living in trees

Many primates live in trees. Instead of paws, primates have hands and feet. Their five-fingered hands are useful for gripping tree branches. Touch the thumb of your right hand to the fingers of your right hand. It is easy, isn't it? You can do this because, like many primates, you have **opposable thumbs**.

Opposable thumbs allow primates to pick up objects. Primates can grab food with their hands and put it in their mouths. They can feel different objects with their sensitive fingertips. Most primates grip with their feet, too. Their big toes are like thumbs, and help them to climb and grasp.

These bonobos are playing with their keeper at a sanctuary in the Democratic Republic of Congo, Africa.

Hands and feet

Primates have other **adaptations** that allow them to make good use of their hands and feet. Instead of claws, primates have flat nails on their thumbs. Some have nails on all their fingers and toes. This allows them to pick up objects more easily than they could with clawed fingers.

Primates can twist their hands and feet in many directions. Two bones in their lower arms and legs allow them to do this. Many animals, such as dogs and cats, walk on their toes. Primates walk on flat feet. They can stand and walk upright.

This spider monkey uses its muscular tail like a fifth hand. It grabs fruits with its hands while it hangs by its tail.

Seeing the world

Primates have forward-facing eyes and excellent depth perception. This means that they can see three-dimensional (3–D) shapes and can judge distances. Primates know how far to reach for the next branch because of their depth perception. They depend more on their sense of sight than on their sense of smell. Because primates rely less on their sense of smell than other mammals, they have smaller, flattened noses.

Primates are intelligent, large-brained animals. They often live together in groups. They protect their young and teach them the skills they will need as adults. Young primates take a long time to grow up. While they are growing, they depend on their mothers for food and protection. Primates grow up slowly, but they live for a long time.

This silverback gorilla is **foraging** for food on the ground. He has found a tasty piece of bamboo.

What are bonobos?

It is hard not to be reminded of people when you watch bonobos. They pout, grin, and make funny faces. They tickle each other and laugh. They use facial expressions and hand gestures to communicate.

Along with chimpanzees, bonobos are our closest relatives. They share more than 98 per cent of their **genes** with people.

This is a family of bonobos, including adults, young, and infants.

The unknown ape

Scientists once thought that bonobos were chimpanzees. However, although they do resemble each other, there are many differences. A bonobo's body is more slender. It has red lips and a darker face. Its head is smaller, with smaller ears, a thinner neck, and narrower shoulders. With their long legs, bonobos can stand more upright than chimps. Scientists think their posture resembles *Australopithecus*, an early human ancestor.

HAROLD COOLIDGE

In 1929, Harold Coolidge was studying a skull in a museum. It had been labelled as a young chimpanzee. Coolidge saw that the skull was from an adult, and that it was too small for a chimp. He realized that bonobos must be a separate **species**. In 1933, they were recognized as such.

This mother and baby are chimpanzees. Can you see how they look different from the bonobos on page 8?

How are bonobos classified?

When scientists **classify** living things, they place them in groups. Members of a group are related to one another and share certain characteristics. For example, you have more things in common with **mammals** than you do with animals in other groups, such as birds or fish.

Mammals are divided into many smaller groups. One of these groups is primates. Primates are further divided into six groups: lemurs; lorises, pottos, and bush babies; tarsiers; New World monkeys; Old World monkeys; and apes. Bonobos are a kind of ape.

Meet the apes

Within the apes, there are six further groups. These groups are gibbons, gorillas, chimpanzees, bonobos, humans, and orangutans. Gibbons belong to a group called the lesser apes. Gorillas, chimpanzees, bonobos, humans, and orangutans form the group known as the great apes. Orangutans split off from other great apes about 12 to 15 million years ago. Later, gorillas became a separate group. The group that was left eventually split off into three: humans, bonobos, and chimpanzees.

BONOBO RELATIVES

For thousands of years, people living in the forests of the Congo in Africa have respected and loved bonobos. They used to tell stories about how bonobos and people were once brothers.

About 5 to 8 million years ago, humans became a separate group. Bonobos and chimpanzees divided into two **species** more recently. Some scientists think this occurred between 690,000 and 900,000 years ago. Others say it may have been 1.8 million years ago. The Congo River in Africa, which formed about 1.5 million years ago, may have separated the two groups. The river still keeps bonobos and chimpanzees apart.

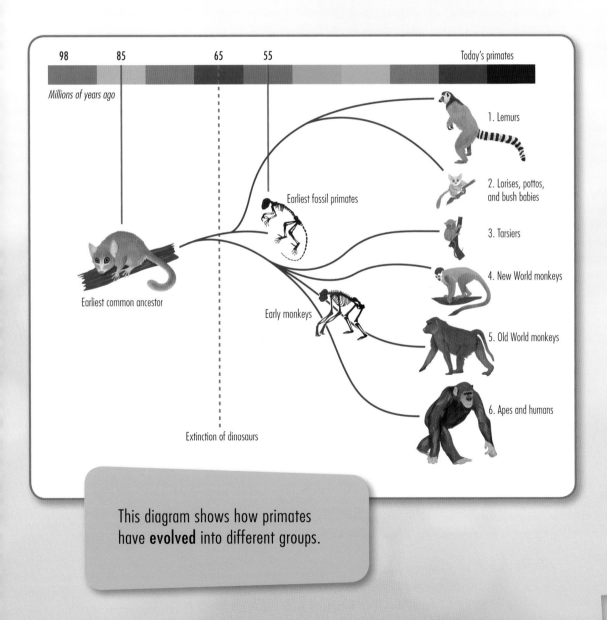

98   85   65   55   Today's primates

Millions of years ago

Earliest fossil primates

Earliest common ancestor

Early monkeys

Extinction of dinosaurs

1. Lemurs

2. Lorises, pottos, and bush babies

3. Tarsiers

4. New World monkeys

5. Old World monkeys

6. Apes and humans

This diagram shows how primates have **evolved** into different groups.

Where do bonobos live?

A **habitat** is the place where an animal lives. Bonobos are found in the Democratic Republic of Congo, in Africa, in a region called the Congo Basin. Three rivers border their habitat: the River Congo to the north and west; the River Kasai to the south; and the River Lualaba to the east. Many rivers run through the Basin, separating the various populations of bonobos.

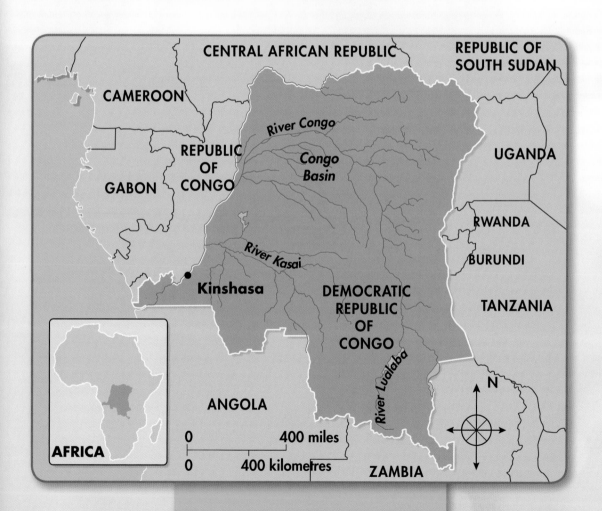

Bonobos live in the Congo Basin, south of the Congo River.

In the rainforest

The Congo Basin contains the second largest **tropical rainforest** on Earth and most of this region is swampy forest. It is warm and humid all year round. The average temperature is 26–28°C (79–82°F). Rain falls throughout the year, except during the dry season. There are also wetlands, grasslands, flooded forests, and farms. Bonobos look for food in all these places.

Leopards, forest elephants, okapi, and other rare animals also live in the Congo Basin. One thousand bird **species**, 400 **mammal** species, and 700 fish species inhabit the Congo Basin. There are probably more than 10,000 kinds of plants. Chimpanzees and gorillas live north of the River Congo. The forest here has more species than most places on Earth, but still fewer than other tropical rainforests.

Rainforests are kept relatively cool by shade from the trees.

What adaptations help bonobos survive?

Have you ever climbed to the top of a tree? You need strong arms and legs to pull yourself up. A strong grip helps you hold on to branches. You must use your balance, and plan the best route to reach the top.

Leaping and swinging

Bonobos not only climb trees, they leap and swing across branches. They have many **adaptations** that help them survive in their forest **habitat**.

Bonobos have **opposable thumbs** as well as opposable big toes. They can grip branches and vines with their hands and feet. They can pick up small objects such as caterpillars and seeds. They can even pick fruit with their toes!

Here you can see a bonobo's opposable big toe.

Bonobos use all four limbs to scramble up and down trees. They swing across long branches, reaching with one strong arm and then the other. Long, narrow shoulder blades allow their arms to swing with ease. They can travel long distances without touching the ground. Bonobos' slender bodies make them more acrobatic than chimpanzees in trees. Bonobos use their climbing skills to reach fruit high up in the treetops. Often they climb as high as 50 metres (164 feet) to pick ripe fruits.

This bonobo is swinging from branch to branch, while her infant clings to her stomach.

Tree travel

Bonobos need excellent balance to travel in trees. They cross thick branches on all fours, walking on their knuckles.

With their long legs, bonobos are also able to walk upright. Their long feet and thigh bones help them balance. More of their weight is in the lower part of their body. This means they can walk upright across wide branches, carrying food in their arms.

On the ground

Bonobos' strong legs allow them to leap from higher branches to lower ones. They leap and dive between trees. When frightened, bonobos jump down from the trees on to the ground. If there is danger beneath a tree, they scurry away on branches before leaping to the ground.

During the dry season, bonobos must travel further to find food. Then they do most of their feeding and travelling on the ground. Bonobos move faster on the ground, as they run on all four limbs.

This bonobo is gathering sugar cane that has been cut by people. He can stand upright and grasp the cane, just like a human being.

Group living

Bonobos are social, which means they live in groups. This behaviour is another adaptation that helps them to survive. Group members find food together and share it with each other. They care for and protect their young together, and warn each other about danger. At night, they nest together in the safety of the trees.

BONOBO BABYSITTER

A 12-year-old male bonobo named Nyota acted as a babysitter to his 4-month-old cousin. When Nyota was young, a male bonobo often cared for him. In turn, as an adult, Nyota spent many days grooming his baby cousin.

Bonobos survive by living in groups and helping each other.

What do bonobos eat?

A flying squirrel gnaws on fruits high up in a tree. A bonobo watches it silently from the ground. Suddenly, the bonobo leaps up the tree and grabs the squirrel. Tree, squirrel, and bonobo are all connected to each other in a relationship called a food chain.

Bonobos are omnivores, which means they eat both plants and animals. They eat many different foods so they belong to many food chains. Many connected food chains add up to a food web. The more connections in a food web, the less affected it will be if one member of it dies out.

These bonobos have spotted something delicious up in a tree.

Favourite foods

Fruit can make up more than half of a bonobo's diet. Bonobos will climb up very high trees to reach these fruits. When they find them, they eat the flesh and seeds.

Bonobos eat over 113 different plants. Leaves, bark, stems, roots, flowers, and seeds are all on the menu. They also eat mushrooms, honey, and soil. Animal food forms a smaller part of their diet. Bonobos catch insects, including caterpillars, bees, butterflies, and beetles. They dig for grubs, earthworms, millipedes, and termites. Bonobos capture small antelope, squirrels, and bats. Groups of bonobos may even hunt monkeys.

It is thought that leopards and pythons may hunt bonobos, but this has not actually been observed. People are the main predators of bonobos.

Bonobos scoop up water to drink from rivers and streams.

What is a bonobo's life cycle?

A young bonobo sits on a tree branch, watching his mother eat. He climbs on to her lap and tastes a bit of fruit. Like all **mammals**, a bonobo depends on its mother when it is young. It becomes more independent as it grows and matures.

The life cycle of an animal covers its birth to its death and all the different stages in between. A bonobo's life cycle begins with mating. Female bonobos may mate with every male in their group. The father of an infant is not known. Female bonobos are pregnant for eight months before giving birth to a single baby.

This newborn bonobo is entirely dependent on its mother.

Baby bonobos

Bonobo mothers take good care of their babies. For the first three months of a baby's life, it never leaves its mother. The baby clings to the mother's belly, and drinks her milk.

By the time it is six months old, the baby starts to creep away. However, it does not go further than about 1 metre (3 feet) from its mother. At around 10 months of age, a baby may crawl as far as 4 metres (13 feet) away. If it goes any further, the mother brings the baby back to her side. At the age of one, a bonobo will begin to walk on four legs.

NEST BUILDING

Mother bonobos build night time nests that they share with their young. Every night, they climb up into the trees and build a new nest.

Bonobos will spend about four minutes building a night time nest. During the day, they also build day nests for the young to rest in. These will usually take less than a minute to construct.

A bonobo may build 19,000 nests during its life!

Growing up

For the first year of its life, a baby's only food is its mother's milk. It might put fruit in its mouth, but it does not actually eat it. As it grows a little older, the baby starts to try new foods. However, it will keep drinking its mother's milk until the age of four or five.

Around the age of two, a young bonobo begins to play. By three, a bonobo has learned to walk and climb almost as well as an adult. Even so, it stays near its mother. Instead of clinging to her front, it rides on her back.

A bonobo stays near its mother for the first four or five years of life. Like all great apes, bonobos have a long childhood.

Young bonobos love to play.

Leaving mum

Around the age of six or seven, female bonobos spend less and less time with their mothers. However, they continue to travel around in the same group as her, looking for food.

At eight years, females wander between different bonobo groups. They settle into a new group between the ages of 9 and 13. Male bonobos continue to grow until they are 14–16 years of age. They stay in their mother's group even when they are fully grown.

A female bonobo has her first baby between the ages of 13 and 14. She gives birth every four to six years. During her lifetime, she will have five to six babies. A bonobo can live to around 50 to 55.

This female bonobo is very old.

How do bonobos behave?

Wild bonobos have not been studied as much as other apes and many things about them are still a mystery to us. Most of what we know about them comes from observing them in zoos. Their behaviour in the wild may be very different.

Looking for food

We do know that bonobos live together in groups. The size of a group ranges from 30 to 80 bonobos. Each day, the group divides up into smaller parties that travel together to look for food. These **foraging** parties can include just a few members or, when fruit is plentiful, 20 or more may band together. Mothers and their children will forage together and sometimes males and females will, too.

This foraging party has found some fruit.

Sleeping

At night, the parties come together again. They choose the trees where they will spend the night. The forest becomes filled with their high-pitched squeals. They build new night nests, about 7 to 15 metres (23 to 49 feet) above the ground. They weave flexible branches together, then stamp them down. They fill the nest with leaves and twigs.

Bonobos groom each other, eat, and play in their nests while settling down for the night. When they fall asleep, bonobos look completely relaxed. They lie on their backs, holding on to a branch with just one foot. Baby bonobos sleep in a nest with their mothers. Adults sometimes sleep together, too. Bonobos are the only apes that share nests as adults.

This bonobo has settled down for the night in a new nest.

Crossing paths

During the day, one foraging party may cross paths with another from a different group. When two groups meet, there is a lot of excitement. Males may chase each other and bark. Females hug and groom each other. They use physical contact to reduce stress and conflict.

These females are grooming each other. Grooming helps them to create good relationships.

Females rule

Females within a group have strong bonds and cooperate well with each other. A band of females will sometimes keep males away from food. The sons of high-ranked females become leaders among the males. While females take care of the young, the males help protect them. When there is danger near by, males will alert the others by barking.

Some scientists believe that bonobo societies are more peaceful than chimpanzee societies. Bonobos are more likely to share food and play with each other. Other scientists think that the differences between bonobos and chimpanzees are related to their **habitats**. Bonobos may fight less because they live in forests where food tends to be plentiful. It is likely that bonobo and chimpanzee groups have many different kinds of social interactions.

GOTTFRIED HOHMANN AND BARBARA FRUTH

Scientists Gottfried Hohmann and Barbara Fruth have been observing bonobos in the wild since 1989. They travel back and forth between Germany and Lomako Forest in the Congo. When they observe bonobos, they try to answer specific questions. For example, in their research about bonobo nests they concluded that females build nests higher in the trees. They learned that females use nests for a longer time than males. Through careful research, they hope to get an accurate picture of bonobo society.

A DAY IN THE LIFE OF A BONOBO

The early morning sun peeks through the leaves in the **rainforest.** High up in a tree, a young bonobo awakes. He hears the high-pitched chatter of the bonobos around him. His mother has already risen from their shared nest. The young bonobo scratches and stretches.

He walks on all fours across a branch. He reaches for a small, hard fruit. As he chews, the fruit skin drops from the corners of his mouth. All around him, other bonobos eat.

Our bonobo follows his mother down, branch by branch, and drops to the ground. His mother joins a group of six other bonobos and they trek away. A few months earlier, he rode on his mother's back. Now, he keeps up on his own.

When the adults stop to eat, he stretches his open hand towards his mother. She hands him a tasty leaf. After he eats, he chases another young bonobo. They roll on the ground and play.

By the middle of the day, he is ready for a rest. His mother quickly builds a day nest. It is not as sturdy as their night nests, but it is fine for a nap. He drinks her milk and then dozes off.

Later in the afternoon, the bonobos file through the woods again. They stop to dig for termites. The youngster pops the wriggling insects into his mouth.

As the sun sets, the bonobo hears loud shrieks. The group has started to assemble. They are building nests for the night. The youngster follows his mother up the tree. After a busy day, he is ready for a rest.

A young bonobo stays close to his mother. He learns how to find food by watching and following her.

How intelligent are bonobos?

When you were younger, an adult might have lain down and lifted you with his or her feet to play "aeroplane". Bonobos play the same game with their babies! Just as humans do, bonobos learn to cooperate and compete with one another through play.

Bonobos are among the most intelligent of non-human primates. Their societies are complex, so the young must learn many different social behaviours.

They play some of the same games that human children play. They chase and tickle each other, and tumble together. They climb up trees and jump to the ground. They make silly faces at each other.

Adult bonobos and their young play together just as humans do.

Communication

Bonobos use facial expressions to tell other bonobos about their moods. These expressions can show whether they are feeling playful, relaxed, or aggressive. They use gentle pats to reassure each other. A begging gesture can be used to ask for support in a fight. The same gesture can be used to ask for food.

Gestures are often combined with sounds. Different sounds alert bonobos to food, threats, and the presence of others. Some scientists think that human communication may have begun with similar gestures.

After **foraging** in small groups, bonobo troops reunite at the end of the day. Scientists think they may exchange information about where to find food. We have much to learn about their communication.

These young bonobos are communicating by making funny faces!

Tool use in captivity

One of the main ways that scientists judge the intelligence of primates is by tool use. Tools such as spears and axes have helped human societies to hunt and build. Today, people use tools for almost every activity. Other primates have also learned to use tools to help them survive.

In zoos and in sanctuaries, bonobos are known to use tools. A bonobo will put a nut on a fallen log, pick up a rock, then use it to crack open the hard husk to reach the soft nut inside. Bonobos also use sticks to pull on objects that are out of reach. They make tools for scooping water and pulling termites out of mounds.

Tool use shows that bonobos can solve problems, such as how to crack open a nut.

Scientists wondered if bonobos could make sharp stone tools similar to the ones made by early humans. They showed Kanzi, a bonobo raised by humans, sharp flakes of stone that he could use to cut string. Kanzi eventually invented a way to make his own flakes.

Tool use in the wild

Unlike chimpanzees, bonobos have not been observed using tools to get food in the wild. This may be because food is plentiful, or because people have not studied bonobos enough to observe it. Bonobos do use tools for other purposes, however. They shoo away bees with leafy branches and they bend shrubs to the ground to sit on them like a leafy cushion.

SUE SAVAGE-RUMBAUGH

Sue Savage-Rumbaugh studies ape to human communication at the Great Ape Trust in Iowa, USA. She has known Kanzi, an adult bonobo, his entire life. When Kanzi was an infant, Sue tried to teach his mother to communicate with a keyboard. The keyboard had symbols that stood for different words. Kanzi's mother never mastered the keyboard. However, Kanzi picked up the language by himself. As well as learning 200 symbols, Savage-Rambaugh thinks Kanzi understands more than 3,000 words.

What threats do bonobos face?

Bonobos were once relatively safe because few people went into the dense forests where they live. But over the past 30 years, the number of bonobos in the wild has dropped. Biologists think their populations will decline further over the next 50 years. They list bonobos as **endangered**. This means that bonobos face a high risk of **extinction**. No one is certain how many bonobos live in the wild. Scientists estimate that there are between 29,500 and 50,000. There may even be as few as 10,000 bonobos.

CLAUDINE ANDRÉ

When Claudine André volunteered at Kinshasa Zoo in 1993, an orphaned bonobo was brought there. André saved him, and soon more bonobos were brought to her. Some had been orphaned when their mothers were killed for bushmeat. André opened a sanctuary called Lola Ya Bonobo (Paradise For Bonobos). Today, 15,000 school children visit her sanctuary each year. They learn about the importance of protecting bonobos.

War and wildlife

Bonobos live only in the Democratic Republic of Congo. The country experienced 10 years of civil war, ending in 2003. This war harmed people and bonobos. Over 4 million people died. Many people were left without their families and became very poor.

At one time, people in the Congo honoured bonobos. They told a legend about a man who had fallen in the forest. He was saved by a bonobo who showed the man where to find food. Local people who told this story had a taboo against hunting bonobos. During the war, some people began to hunt animals for their meat, known as bushmeat. Many bonobos were killed.

Smoked bonobo meat is sold at markets like this one.

Poaching

Poaching (illegal hunting) is the greatest threat to bonobos. As a result of the civil war, more people have guns. Poachers follow new roads into the **rainforests** in which bonobos live. Some poachers hunt and sell bushmeat as a way to survive. They also kill mother bonobos and sell their babies as pets.

PROTECTED OR HUNTED?

Bonobos and other endangered animals are supposed to be protected in Salonga National Park in the Congo. But a recent survey found evidence of hunting in 51 per cent of the park.

Habitat loss

Habitat destruction also harms bonobos. Bonobos need large forests to find food. Illegal logging near bonobo reserves leaves bonobos without enough space. Foreign companies often run these tree-cutting operations. Their profits do not benefit local people, who still hunt bushmeat.

Logging threatens the forests where bonobos live.

Farming also destroys bonobos' habitats. People near rainforests often carry out slash-and-burn agriculture. They clear forests by cutting and burning trees. Mining also clears forests. Coltan is a mineral that is mined in the Congo. It is used in mobile phones, DVD players, video game systems, and computers. Copper, uranium, gold, and diamonds are also mined. Pollution from mining harms people and bonobos.

Disease

Bonobos can catch many human diseases because we are so closely related. Logging roads bring more people into the forests. When people live near bonobos, the risk of spreading diseases increases. Ebola, a disease deadly to humans, now harms gorilla populations in the Congo. It could harm bonobos, too.

Mining pollutes the air and water. It harms habitats for people and bonobos.

How can people help bonobos?

Bonobos are an important part of the **rainforest** in the Congo. They spread tree seeds by eating fruit. They help sustain the rainforest, which is an environment that people need.

People need bonobos

Along with chimpanzees, bonobos are our closest relatives. Studying their societies may reveal how human societies **evolved**. It may also show how we acquired language. People might benefit by understanding how bonobos resolve conflicts without war. For people to learn from and understand these creatures, we must protect bonobos and their **habitat**.

People care about bonobos in part because they remind us of ourselves. These feelings can lead people to get involved in protecting bonobos' habitats.

Understanding how bonobos resolve conflicts might one day help humans live more peacefully.

Taking action

Many people in the Congo and around the world are trying to protect bonobos and the rainforests where they live. In 2005, the Bonobo Peace Forest was created. It is a series of small forest reserves that are linked together. People who live in the reserves manage them. Local people work to protect their culture and the animals of the forest. They learn **sustainable** ways to use the forest resources. This means that they grow food and use forest products in ways that do not put rainforest plants and animals at risk.

LEARNING FROM BONOBOS

Chilean biologist Isabel Behncke Izquierdo studies bonobos in the wild. She thinks that there are three important things people can learn from bonobos: playfulness, social tolerance, and female closeness. Strong friendships between females seem to make bonobos more peaceful and tolerant.

Many people in the Congo work to protect bonobos and the rainforest.

Surveying bonobos

To decide how to protect bonobos, people must know where bonobos live. Many organizations are working to survey bonobo populations in the rainforest. Their goal is to estimate the number of bonobos, and find where they feed and nest. They measure different characteristics of the forests where bonobos live. They look at the impact of people. Then they develop a plan to **conserve** the forest.

Some surveys are being done in the Congo's Salonga National Park. This is the largest **tropical** forest national park in Africa. It has been named a World Heritage Site, recognizing it as one of the world's most important natural places.

SANKURU NATURE RESERVE

In November 2007, the Democratic Republic of Congo announced plans for a huge nature reserve. Called the Sankuru Nature Reserve, it is about the size of Belgium. The creation of this nature reserve means that more than 10 per cent of the land in the country is protected. The Sankuru Nature Reserve is home to bonobos, forest elephants, and other rare **mammals**. Helping people in Sankuru find ways to make a living other than the bushmeat trade is the first step for managing the new reserve.

Surveyors in Salonga National Park compare current bonobo populations with those before the civil war. Years of war have left Congolese people with few ways to survive. Many have turned to illegal hunting and logging. Park workers are trying to stop the poaching of bonobos and other **endangered** animals. They teach people the value of the rainforest and the animals that live there.

Guards patrol rivers surrounding Salonga National Park to stop poachers from entering the park.

What does the future hold for bonobos?

The future for bonobos is uncertain. Poaching and **habitat** destruction must be stopped for bonobos to survive. Because bonobos have only one baby at a time, illegal hunting has a huge impact on their numbers.

Bonobos and people

After years of civil war, many people who live in the Democratic Republic of Congo are very poor. In order for bonobos to survive, people who live in and near their habitats also need help. Teaching people how to use forest resources without destroying them is critical. Congolese field biologists and park workers must be well trained so they can lead their country's conservation efforts.

Because bonobos have not been known to science for as long as other apes, people know less about these fascinating creatures. Many people have never heard of bonobos. People in the Congo and around the world must learn about bonobos and the importance of protecting them.

Many groups are working to save bonobos and their habitats. You can help bonobos by teaching others about them. The more people know about bonobos, the more they will want to make sure that bonobos and their habitats survive.

Bonobos thrive in protected forests where they are not hunted.

SALLY JEWELL COXE

Sally Jewell Coxe is the president and co-founder of the Bonobo Conservation Initiative. For 10 years, her group has worked to **conserve** bonobos and their habitats. Together with Congolese communities and the government, she has helped create new protected areas for bonobos. The group's education programmes promote traditional Congolese beliefs and culture. Respect for the animals of the **rainforest** is taught through Congolese stories and songs.

Bonobo profile

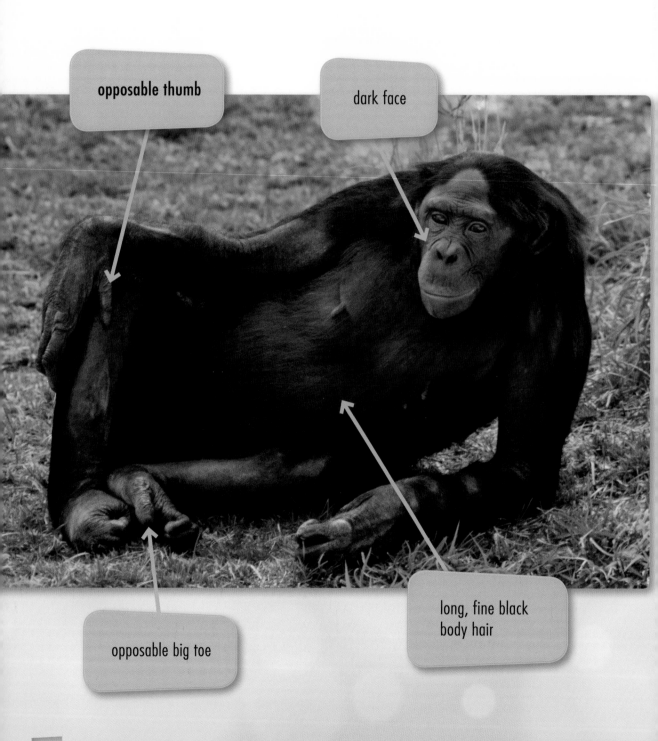

opposable thumb

dark face

opposable big toe

long, fine black body hair

Species: *Pan paniscus*

Weight: adult males 45 kilograms (99 pounds); adult females 33 kilograms (73 pounds)

Height [from head to rump]: 70–90 centimetres (28–35 inches)

Habitat: rainforests of the Congo Basin

Diet: fruits, leaves, seeds, flowers, honey, eggs, soil, mushrooms, grubs, squirrel, antelope, monkeys

Number of young: one infant born after 8 months of pregnancy. Females will give birth every 4–6 years after they have reached maturity at 13–14 years.

Life expectancy: 50–55 years

Glossary

adaptation body part or behaviour of a living thing that helps it survive in a particular habitat

classify group living things together by their similarities and differences

conserve protect from harm or destruction

endangered living thing that is at risk of dying out

evolve change gradually over time

extinct living thing that has died out

extinction when a type of living thing has died out

forage look for food over a wide area

gene information that is passed from parent to young and which determines species, as well as other characteristics

habitat natural environment of a living thing

mammal animal that has fur or hair, gives birth to live young, and feeds its young on milk from the mother

opposable thumb thumb that can face and touch the fingers on the same hand

rainforest forest with tall, thickly-growing trees in an area with high rainfall

species group of similar living things that can mate with each other

sustainable able to be kept going over a long period of time

tropical regions of Earth around the equator

Find out more

Books

100 Things You Should Know About Monkeys and Apes, Camilla
de la Bedoyere (Miles Kelly, 2008)

Classifying Living Things: Classifying Mammals, Andrew Solway
(Raintree, 2009)

Protecting Food Chains: Rainforest Food Chains, Heidi Moore
(Raintree, 2010)

Websites

www.bristolzoo.org.uk/mammals
Visit this website to find out lots more about mammals.

www.bbc.co.uk/nature/life/Bonobo
Learn about bonobos and other primates on this BBC website.

Organizations to contact

World Wildlife Fund UK
www.wwf.org.uk
WWF works to protect animals and nature, and needs your help!
Have a look at their website and see what you can do.

Endangered Species International
www.endangeredspeciesinternational.org/index.php
This organization focuses on saving endangered animals
around the world.

Durrell Wildlife Conservation Trust
www.durrell.org
This organization aims to help save animal species from extinction.

Index

Attack and Defence

KINGFISHER

First published 2011 by Kingfisher
an imprint of Macmillan Children's Books
a division of Macmillan Publishers Limited
20 New Wharf Road, London N1 9RR
Basingstoke and Oxford

Associated companies throughout the world
www.panmacmillan.com

A CIP catalogue record for this book is available
from the British Library.

Conceived and produced by
Weldon Owen Pty Ltd
59–61 Victoria Street, McMahons Point
Sydney NSW 2060, Australia
weldonowenpublishing.com

Copyright © 2011 Weldon Owen Pty Ltd

WELDON OWEN PTY LTD
Managing Director Kay Scarlett
Publisher Corinne Roberts
Creative Director Sue Burk
**Senior Vice President,
International Sales** Stuart Laurence
Sales Manager, North America Ellen Towell
**Administration Manager,
International Sales** Kristine Ravn

Managing Editor Helen Bateman
Consultant Professor Phil Whitfield
Design Concept Cooling Brown Ltd
Designer Michelle Cutler
Images Manager Trucie Henderson
Production Director Todd Rechner
Production and Prepress Controller Mike Crowton

ISBN 978-0-7534-3381-2

Printed and bound in China by 1010 Printing Int Ltd.

The paper used in the manufacture of this book is
sourced from wood grown in sustainable forests.
It complies with the Environmental Management
System Standard ISO 14001:2004

A WELDON OWEN PRODUCTION

animalplanet.co.uk
animalplanetbooks.com

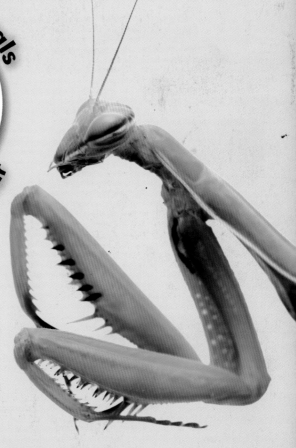

Weird and Wonderful

Attack and Defence

Kathy Riley

Astonishing Animals

Bizarre Behaviour

KINGFISHER

Contents

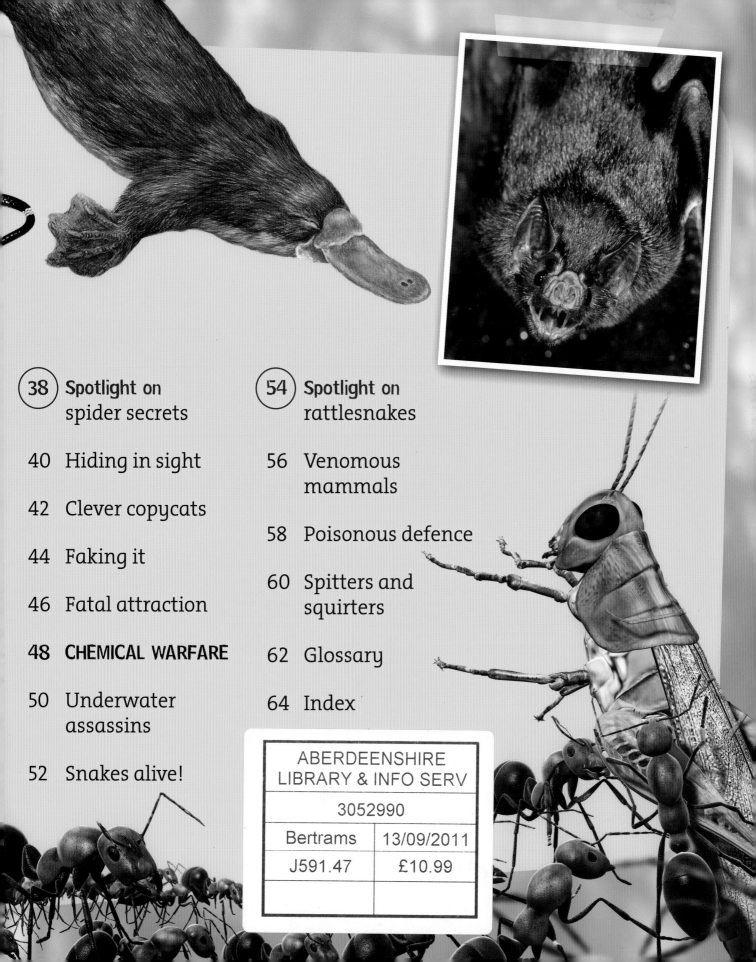

WEAPONS AND TOOLS

Animals are equipped with a variety of built-in weapons and tools to help them survive: from razor-sharp teeth and claws, impenetrable body armour and powerful muscles to toxic saliva, electricity and poisonous body parts. These weapons and tools can make even the smallest creature a formidable and deadly opponent.

A long-tailed pangolin shows off its body armour.

Jaws of death

Chomping, chewing, puncturing, tearing, grinding and cutting – these are just a few of the tasks that predatory animals need their teeth and jaws to perform. Their teeth come in all shapes and sizes, each specially designed for its job. Some animals' mouths have extra hidden weapons, such as deadly saliva.

Shark attack

The great white shark has the largest and most fearsome teeth of all the world's sharks. Each tooth is serrated and as sharp as a saw blade.

A great white shark lunges up from below, its massive teeth bared and ready to bite down on its prey.

Dirty tricks The Komodo dragon is the world's largest lizard. Its deadliest weapon is the bacteria in its saliva. Once bitten, the dragon's prey slowly dies of blood poisoning.

Specialized teeth A tiger has big canine teeth for killing, small front incisors for plucking feathers or fur and cheek teeth for ripping meat off bones and chomping it into chunks.

Animal facts

1 Dolphins keep the same set of teeth for their whole lives.

2 Tusks are very long teeth. About one third of an elephant's tusk is hidden inside its head.

3 A shark is continually growing new sets of teeth. Every time the shark loses a tooth, a new one moves forward to take its place.

Nifty fingers

We would be lost without the use of our fingers and hands, and so would many other creatures in the animal kingdom. Whether they are needed for slashing, grasping, climbing, digging, cutting, plucking or piercing, animals' claws and talons are vitally important for their survival.

Powerful grasp An owl swoops down with toes and sharp talons ready to close around its victim. Its feet can lock in and hold prey for hours without tiring.

Hungry bear Grizzly bears use their strong claws to dig into burrows; strike down large animals such as moose; pluck fish from rivers and forage for insects, fruit and plants.

Nail it Shown here in real size, a bear's claw is powerful and versatile. It can perform many different jobs – from holding and digging to cutting, ripping and slashing.

← 10 centimetres →

Big, powerful, crushing claws

Slender fingers and sharp nails

Designer digits

Whether performing delicate tasks such as picking berries and extracting insects, or destructive jobs such as crushing prey, animals' claws are cleverly designed to meet their needs.

Pincer attack Lobsters have oversized crusher claws and smaller pincer claws for attacking and tearing apart their prey.

Insect excavator The aye-aye from Madagascar has a long, spindly middle finger for extracting grubs from tree holes.

Rock star The marine iguana, which is found along the coast of the Galápagos Islands, has long, curved claws, which help it grip on to rocks in heavy seas.

Animal facts

1 The osprey, a type of raptor, can reverse its outer toe to allow it to grab and carry a fish using two claws in front and two behind.

2 A lobster can drop a claw and grow back another one.

3 Koalas and some primates, including humans and gorillas, are the only animals with fingerprints.

Spotlight on

Creepy-crawly A centipede is small, but ferocious. It is carnivorous and has poisonous claws behind its mouth that can trap and paralyse prey.

little monsters

In the animal kingdom, small does not necessarily mean weak. Poison, camouflage, well-developed senses and finely tuned physical characteristics are just some of the weapons these miniature hunters use to rule their domain. Sometimes being small is a great advantage in itself, as it means escaping detection until the last possible moment.

Sting operation Scorpions are menacing creatures with large, snapping pincers and a stinging tail that whips around to deliver a fatal dose of poison to small animals.

Mighty pincers trap or crush prey in their grasp.

Ambush artist Folding its spiny forelegs as if in prayer, the praying mantis sits camouflaged on a branch until an unsuspecting victim approaches. Then it pounces with fierce precision.

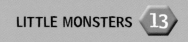

Funnel-web spider

With solid, black, hairy bodies, aggressive natures, and fangs as sharp and deadly as pickaxes, Australia's funnel-web spiders are among the most dangerous and venomous spiders in the world.

Attack mode This funnel-web spider is ready to strike. It cannot see with its head back; instead, it responds to vibrations. Its venom contains a chemical called atracotoxin, which can kill humans.

The pedipalps, next to the mouth, aid in eating food.

Deadly venom travels through ducts in the fangs.

Tiny hairs on the spider's body pick up smells, sounds and vibrations.

The **big** squeeze

Pythons and boas are the largest living snakes in the world, and they have a unique method of attack: they wrap their long body around prey and use their powerful muscles to squeeze it to death. Then they eat their victim whole. Digesting a large animal can take weeks or even months.

Quick lunge The emerald tree boa from South America catches prey with its long teeth, pulls it in and then asphyxiates it.

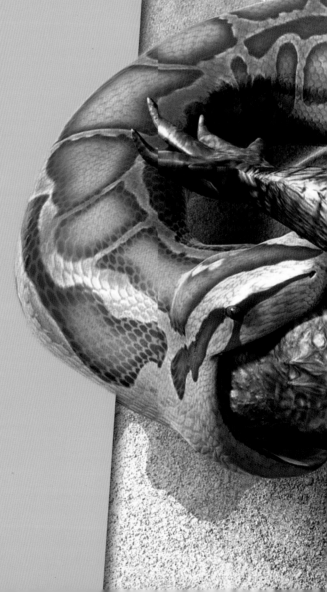

Last gasp

Contrary to what many people think, constrictors do not kill their prey by crushing it. Rather, they tighten their grip every time the victim breathes out. Gradually, the victim suffocates.

The Amazon tree boa anchors itself around a tree branch, leaving its front end free to strike out at prey.

Death hug A young Siamese crocodile is no match for a hungry Burmese python. These pythons can grow to 6 metres and weigh 45 kilograms.

What is the main difference between a python and a boa?

Animal facts

❶ Pythons and boas are the only snakes with remnant hind limbs. These limbs are known as anal spurs.

❷ The longest snake in the world is the reticulated python, which regularly reaches lengths of more than 6.25 metres.

❸ Pythons and boas move the bones in their jaws apart to eat their prey whole.

A: A boa gives birth to live young, whereas a python lays eggs.

Suits of armour

Sometimes the best defence is an impenetrable outer layer – one that is so tough an attacker soon gives up and moves on to an easier target. Spikes, shells, scales and thick hides are a few examples of the body armour worn by animals to protect them from predators.

Spines move to help urchins change direction.

Prickly customer
Sea urchins belong to a group called echinoderms, from the Greek word for 'spiny-skinned'. Many sea urchin species have venom in their spines for extra protection.

Body armour The armadillo's head and back are covered with a flexible carapace of bony plates covered with horny skin. Its belly, however, is soft and vulnerable.

Pangolin protection

A pangolin, also known as a scaly anteater, has very sharp scales. When attacked, it will roll into a tight ball that is almost impossible to unroll.

Although it looks like a reptile, a pangolin is actually a mammal.

Overlapping scales

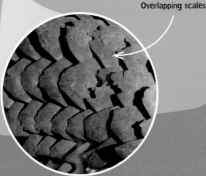

Little bug The woodlouse is sometimes called the armadillo bug because of its resemblance to a tiny armadillo. It is a land-dwelling crustacean.

ZOOM IN

Watch out, these spines can hurt!

All puffed up Pufferfish defend themselves by inflating with water or air to try to appear larger. Their spines are stiff, pointed and very sharp.

Each spine is sharp and hollow.

Spiky hairdo An echidna's spines are actually modified hairs. When threatened, it will curl into a ball or burrow into the ground.

Horned and dangerous A rhinoceros's horn is made up of fibrous keratin. This, together with its incredibly tough skin, makes it very well protected.

Blood thirsty

These creatures might be small, but they are perfectly designed for finding and feasting on their favourite food: blood! Many carry anaesthetic in their saliva, so the host animal does not feel them until they have had their fill. Some are harmless, but some carry diseases that can be dangerous to humans.

Bleeding machine Leeches are mighty clever at getting their meals – chemicals in their saliva stop their host's blood from clotting. This helps increase blood flow and anaesthetize the bite site, so they can feast in peace.

One tick can lay up to 3,000 eggs!

🐾 Animal facts

1 A tick can ingest up to 100 times its own body weight in blood.

2 Leeches are sometimes used on human patients, to help reduce swelling and restore blood flow after microsurgery.

3 Only adult female mosquitoes bite humans and other animals. Male mosquitoes feed on nectar and other sources of sugar.

An adult bedbug is about the size of an apple seed.

Human hitchhikers Bedbugs and ticks love human blood. Bedbugs can cause rashes and itchy bites, whereas ticks are more dangerous, sometimes carrying diseases or causing paralysis in animals.

A bedbug's skin-piercing mouthparts

Fish parasite

The candiru is a tiny catfish from the Amazon. It swims in through the gills of other fish and feeds on their blood. It can also swim up the urethra of a bathing human!

Little Dracula Vampire bats are found in the Americas, where they hunt at night for warm-blooded animals. Rather than sucking blood, they bite prey then lick blood from the wound.

Vampire bats sometimes feed on human blood!

Shocking hunters

Electricity is used by many animals for a number of different purposes. Some fish use echolocation – they emit pulses that set up an electric field in the water. They use these pulses to work out where their prey is. Others use electrical signals to communicate with each other. Many will use electricity to deliver a nasty shock that can stun or kill.

Stargazer fish If you spot this strange face in the sandy seabed, do not touch it. Poisonous spines behind the stargazer's pectoral fins can deliver electric shocks.

 Animal facts

❶ Electroreception (see panel, page 21) works better for aquatic animals because water conducts electricity more effectively than air.

❷ Sharks detect the electrical fields of potential prey using pores beneath their snout, called the ampullae of Lorenzini.

❸ The biggest recorded shock produced by an electric eel is 650 volts, enough to stun a horse.

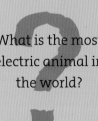 What is the most electric animal in the world?

A marbled torpedo ray arches its back, ready to deliver a shock.

Electric navigation

All animals produce electrical impulses, but not all animals can sense them. Electroreception is the word used to describe the ability to detect electrical fields, which animals do using special nerves called electroreceptors.

Stun gun This bullseye electric ray is one of 40 species of electric rays that stun prey by delivering electric shocks from organs behind their eyes.

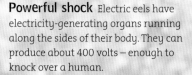

The platypus and echidna are the only mammals that can detect electrical signals. The platypus has thousands of electroreceptors in its bill.

Powerful shock Electric eels have electricity-generating organs running along the sides of their body. They can produce about 400 volts — enough to knock over a human.

Electroreceptors in the echidna's little snout can pick up minute electric pulses produced by moving prey.

TEAM SPIRIT

Survival is a game of numbers for many animals. When they join forces, they increase their chance of finding food and mates and avoiding attack. Whether it is a graceful pod of dolphins or a seething horde of army ants, a coordinated team of animals is a force to be reckoned with.

Common dolphins live in large groups as a defence against predators.

Pack attack

One wolf is no match for a massive moose, but eight wolves make a truly fearsome team. Many animals – in particular canids, or doglike carnivores – often work together to mount effective and lethal attacks against prey. Sometimes two different species will team up, each bringing its own unique talents to the group.

Tag teams A pride of lions brings down the prey. Once the lions have finished eating, a pack of hyenas arrives to finish the job.

Strategic hunt Wolves are far more effective at hunting large prey if they work together. A mother caribou cannot defend herself and her calf against a coordinated attack.

The wolves stealthily sneak up on the caribou without being seen.

After giving chase, the wolves pinpoint the caribou calf as their chosen target.

Panicked and confused, the caribou calf tries to run and is caught by the wolves.

Animal facts

1 Wolves can run as fast as 64 kilometres per hour over short distances.

2 African hunting dogs roam in packs of up to 40 members.

3 Dog packs have a strict social hierarchy, with an alpha, or top, male and female. The alpha dogs are the only ones allowed to breed.

Team effort Grey wolves will tirelessly chase a moose until it falters. Then they attack swiftly, each wolf biting a different part of the doomed animal.

Water warfare

Whales, dolphins and porpoises, which belong to the order Cetacea, are highly sociable animals. They have a wide variety of intelligent methods for hunting in groups, which are mesmerizing to watch. From a slippery school of fish to a formidable great white shark, no challenge is too great for these determined teams!

Synchronized swimmers

Dolphins work together to catch a school of fish. One dolphin swims in circles around the school, herding it towards the other dolphins, who are waiting for their fishy feast.

A pod of hungry dolphins works together to make an easy meal out of this large school of fish.

Animal facts

❶ A pod of humpback whales can perform bubblenet feeding, where they create a tightening 'net' of bubbles around a school of fish, before devouring them.

❷ Grouper fish and moray eels hunt cooperatively for prey. Groupers chase prey in the open ocean; when the prey hides in a crevice, the eels flush them out.

❸ Common dolphins can form very large groups of sometimes thousands at a time.

A lone great white
is no match for a
pod of orcas.

Killer move Intelligent and deadly,
a pod of orcas, or killer whales, can
overcome a great white shark by driving
it to the surface and immobilizing it by
flipping it upside down.

The 1.7-metre Humboldt squid hunts

in groups of up to 1,200 for small fish and krill.

Mob mentality

An immense group of animals is a dramatic and spectacular sight. A swarm of krill can cover 5 kilometres of ocean, flocks of tropical birds make noisy and colourful clouds and insects often congregate in mind-boggling numbers. Animals swarm to increase their chance of surviving, mating or feeding.

ZOOM IN

Piranha frenzy Churning water and the flash of scales is all you will see when piranhas attack in a large group, all biting their prey at the same time.

Brutal bite Powerful jaws and razor-sharp teeth can shred the flesh of large prey in minutes. Native South American people use piranha teeth to make weapons and tools.

Midges on the move

If you see a thick cloud of midges hovering mid-air, it is mating season. Male midges congregate to attract females, who mate with them and then leave to lay their eggs.

Midges usually swarm at dusk during warmer months.

Why do bees swarm?

Locust army A swarm of locusts can travel up to 500 kilometres in one night, descending in their millions and stripping foliage from vast areas.

A: To protect the queen bee when moving to a new nest.

Spotlight on army ants

Army ants are the absolute masters of attack. These vicious insects form colonies of millions of individuals, which sweep across vast areas and destroy every small living creature in their path. Despite the fact that they are so tiny, they are able to defeat their victims with their aggression and overwhelming numbers.

No escape Hopelessly outnumbered, this grasshopper will be killed by fierce bites and venomous stings, before being dismembered to help feed the colony. Ants use the same weapons against intruders and attackers.

Despite its size, a grasshopper is no match for an aggressive ant army.

Body builders Army ants improvise while they are on the move. They build bridges and nests with their bodies, latching on to each other with their mandibles, or mouthparts, and claws.

Scorpion defeated Army ants are blind and need movement to trigger an attack. This scorpion was doomed the instant it scuttled across the path of an oncoming swarm.

It is the job of the smaller worker ants to attack, kill and cut up prey.

The soldier ants, with their enormous mandibles, are the guards of the colony.

Safety in numbers

Animals are usually safer when they stick together. A zebra has less chance of becoming dinner for a hungry lion if it travels in a group. More pairs of eyes mean more chance of spotting trouble, which is important for fish swimming in murky water or animals made vulnerable by feeding or breeding.

All ashore Sea lions hunt individually but form huge colonies when breeding. A group of seals, sea lions or walrus is called a herd, and a breeding colony is called a rookery.

Group huddle In Antarctica, immense colonies of breeding king penguins stand together for protection against predators such as petrels, which steal eggs and chicks.

School assembly A school of fish has a better chance of finding food and mates. It can spot predators more effectively, and if attacked can split up and create confusion.

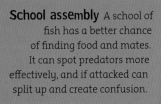

On the lookout

Meerkats live in large, highly organized groups. During the day, some will head out hunting, while others babysit the young or stand guard, barking a warning if they spot danger.

In the Kalahari Desert in South Africa, meerkats take turns to scan the landscape for potential predators.

Animal facts

1 Emperor penguins huddle in groups of up to 5,000 to survive Antarctic winters, which can get as cold as −60°C.

2 When attacked or threatened, a minnow releases a chemical to warn other minnows of the danger.

3 In the Arctic, musk oxen will stand shoulder to shoulder to form a defensive barrier against attack by wolves.

Savannah survival The flat, treeless plains of Africa offer few hiding places for vulnerable animals. By grouping together, animals such as giraffes, zebras, springboks and impalas have a better chance of avoiding attack.

TRICKS AND TRAPS

Sometimes a little bit of trickery goes a long way. Many animals have evolved clever camouflage or costumes to fool would-be attackers or prey. They are also excellent performers, capable of staying as still as a rock, stick or flower, or even striking a pose that makes them appear dead and uninviting to predators.

An orb-weaving spider waits patiently for an insect to fly into its trap.

Dressed to kill

Camouflage is a powerful tool when hunting for a meal. Many creatures blend perfectly into their surroundings, enabling them to sneak up on prey or wait for prey to come to them. Their disguise is so convincing that their victim is totally fooled – right up until the last, fatal moment.

Arctic ghost The snowy owl's stunning white plumage blends in with its Arctic surroundings, which is very useful as it hunts during the day. Its prey includes lemmings, rabbits, rodents, birds and fish.

Deadly stonefish Looking exactly like an algae-covered stone on a rocky reef, the stonefish is extremely dangerous. Spines on its dorsal fin inject the most toxic venom of any fish in the world.

Animal facts

1 Scientists believe wobbegongs have been in our oceans for more than 160 million years.

2 Only the male snowy owl is all white. Female snowy owls are white with dark spots on their wings.

3 Not all camouflage is visual. For example, some animals roll in dung to disguise their scent.

Cunning hunter Wolves are intelligent predators, adapting their hunting methods to their surroundings. This timber wolf crouches low to the ground so the dry grass camouflages its grey fur.

Master of disguise

Masquerading as a flower, this pretty pink orchid mantis evades detection by predators but also attracts insects, which it devours.

Some insects have perfected the art of disguise, with a costume that fools both predator and prey.

Why do killer whales have white undersides?

Wobbegongs have lightning reflexes and dagger-sharp teeth.

Wily wobbegong This shark is full of tricks. Its mottled skin blends in with the sea floor, while the tassels around its snout lure hungry fish. It lies perfectly still until it senses its prey, then pounces.

A: *So sea creatures below cannot see them against the light of the sky.*

Spotlight on

Long jumper Instead of using leg muscles to jump, as humans do, jumping spiders propel themselves by altering the pressure of the liquid inside their body. Their excellent eyesight helps them judge jumping distances.

spider secrets

Spiders have an amazing collection of weapons to help them hunt. Camouflage, sharp fangs, poison, speed, mobility, finely tuned senses and endless streams of strong and versatile silk enable them to overcome prey as small as a fly and as large as a human. This makes them fascinating as well as fearsome.

This spider is making a quick getaway on a strong line of silk called a dragline.

Master weavers

A strand of spider silk is elastic, but as strong as steel. It is incredibly useful. Spiders can use it to bind victims, move around, construct shelters, protect eggs and build many different types of webs.

The scaffold web has vertical threads reaching the ground that trap insects walking past.

When prey blunders into a triangle web, the spider lets go of its end and the web collapses.

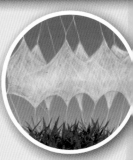

This hammock web traps prey in a sticky maze until it eventually falls on to a platform.

Booby trap The trapdoor spider waits until it feels the vibrations of its prey walking over its hidden door. Then it races up, raises its hatch and pounces.

Scuba spider The diving bell spider builds its underwater home by trapping air inside a silken web. It preys on aquatic animals that pass by. It also goes out hunting, breathing from a thin film of air around its abdomen.

Flower power Some crab spiders can change colours like a chameleon. They sit on top of a flower, blending in perfectly. When an unsuspecting insect comes to collect nectar, it gets a nasty surprise!

Hiding in sight

Whether they live on land or in the sea, in deserts, lush rainforests or snow-covered terrain, many animals use pattern or colour to blend into the background. Cunning camouflage can help a creature avoid attracting the attention of predatory eyes – and becoming a victim.

Sticky surprise With its long, thin body, twiggy legs and motionless posture, the stick insect is hard to spot. It looks like part of a tree branch.

Hiding in the sea

Creatures can go unnoticed on the sandy seabed if they have speckled skin and a flat body and stay relatively still. Among vibrant coral, brighter colours work. Sea dragons are fish that have a different disguise: leafy appendages that look like seaweed.

The leafy sea dragon has yellow-green colouring and 'fins' that look just like trailing seaweed.

Which animal changes colour the fastest?

The sloth moth lays its eggs in the sloth's dung.

Gobies are small fish. Discreet colouring helps them blend into the background.

This leopard flounder has a pattern that looks just like the pebbly ocean floor.

ZOOM IN

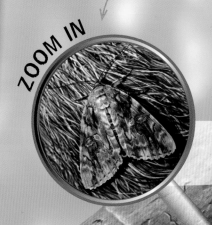

Insect impersonators

Brimstone butterfly
The veined, leaf-shaped wings of this butterfly help it blend in perfectly with its background.

Leaf mimic katydid A pile of dead leaves on the forest floor is the perfect refuge for this insect.

Bark bug When motionless, this little bug is almost impossible to spot against the bark of a tree.

Slothful living The three-toed sloth is a slow-moving tree-dweller. Green algae grows on its coat, helping to camouflage it within the leafy canopy.

The **sloth moth** lives in the sloth's shaggy fur.

A: *The cuttlefish.*

Clever copycats

Many animals defend themselves by using mimicry to trick predators or prey into thinking they are something else. Some display the same colours or patterns as a dangerous, poisonous or bad-tasting animal. Others have a body part that makes it looks like another animal, which confuses or startles attackers and gives the animal a chance to escape.

Can you spot the differences between this ant and the spider below?

Ant or spider? The spider below is masquerading as a weaver ant. Weaver ants have a terrible taste and painful bite, so the spider's disguise fools predators into thinking it is just another unappetising ant.

Why do male cuttlefish sometimes mimic female cuttlefish?

Black patches on the spider's head look like ant eyes.

The harmless milk snake copies the colours of the poisonous coral snake for protection.

Fake owl-eyes startle predators when the moth opens its wings.

Watchful wings

Eyespots on the wings of the polyphemus silk moth (far left) look just like the fierce gaze of an owl (left). The moth uses its spots to scare away hungry birds.

Copying this owl's piercing gaze is a clever survival strategy.

Animals recognize the colours of the nasty yellow jacket wasp and stay away.

Red, black and yellow bands of the coral snake warn enemies of its poison.

The wasp beetle copies the yellow jacket wasp for protection.

Sneaky snakes These two snakes have similar colours and patterns, but the one pictured above is an extremely poisonous coral snake, while the one on the left is a harmless milk snake.

Wasp disguise Predators have learnt that a black-and-yellow pattern indicates a yellow jacket wasp with a nasty sting. They do not realise that this is not a wasp at all, but a clever copycat!

A: So they can mate with females without other males detecting them.

Faking it

When danger looms and escape is impossible, many animals will put on the performance of their life. Some drop their tail or a leg as a decoy or feign injury to distract their attackers. Others simply play dead. The more convincing their act, the better chance they have for survival.

Tricky tail Most lizard species, including geckos, can drop their tail when they are under attack. The tail keeps wriggling like a tasty worm, diverting the attacker's attention while the animal escapes.

The gecko escapes, leaving its wriggling tail behind. It then grows a new tail.

Plover's eggs

What does 'playing possum' mean?

Broken wing Plovers and other ground-nesting birds sometimes fake an injured wing to convince predators they are easy pickings. They flap around on the ground and lead the predator away from their precious nest.

Animal facts

1 The tail of the Australian chameleon gecko not only wriggles after it is dropped, but also squeaks.

2 Lizards and spiders can regenerate their shed legs or tail over a number of weeks.

3 Darwin's frog of South America will jump into a stream and roll on to its back, playing dead while the water carries it away.

Playing dead

Most animals prefer to hunt and eat live prey, so some creatures will play dead to evade the attention of predators. Some will even release a smell similar to rotting meat.

This grass snake might look dead, but once the threat has passed, it will spring to life and slither safely away.

When it senses danger, the opossum feigns death, or 'plays possum'. Its eyes glaze over, its tongue hangs out and its breathing slows down.

The **harvestman** can drop one of

its legs to confuse a predator.

A: *Pretending to be dead, unconscious or asleep.*

Fatal attraction

Not all predators actively seek out their prey. Some have perfected the art of attracting prey to them. With a few nifty tricks – such as clever camouflage and convincing lures – and a great deal of patience, these creatures have managed to take the hard physical work out of finding their next meal.

The heron drops a leaf or twig into the moving stream.

The heron follows its swirling lure downstream.

When a fish swims up to investigate, the hungry heron snatches it up.

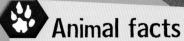 Animal facts

1 The Australian bird-dropping spider looks and smells like bird dung, to attract its favourite food: flies.

2 Margay cats, from Central and South America, sometimes imitate the distress call of a young tamarin monkey to lure adult tamarins.

3 Some snakes use caudal luring to attract prey, wriggling and waving their tail until the prey comes within striking distance.

Bird bait Green herons have developed an innovative way of catching a meal. They carefully select sticks or leaves that are light enough to swirl on the water's surface and attract fish.

Lure

Gone fishing

Anglerfish are slow-moving predators that wait for food to come to them. They dangle a glowing or wormlike lure in front of their cavernous mouth, which draws unsuspecting prey within easy striking distance.

The deep-sea anglerfish uses its bright lure to attract hungry fish in the deep, dark ocean – then gobbles them down.

How does the *Portia* spider lure its spider prey?

Death trap

Perfectly camouflaged by its mud-brown, algae-covered shell, the alligator snapping turtle opens its mouth to reveal a tantalising, wriggling, wormlike tongue. When a hungry fish ventures in ... wham!

A: By plucking out the rhythm of a trapped insect on the spider's web.

CHEMICAL WARFARE

Spines, spurs, saliva, tentacles, fangs, fur and feathers – anything and everything has poisonous potential in the animal kingdom. Creatures use toxins to stun, paralyse or kill outright, making it easier to devour prey or escape from an attacker. Unfortunately for the victim, the danger is often invisible – until it is too late!

A venomous sea krait lurks in the coral reef, ready to ambush prey.

Underwater assassins

Forget about sharks – the most deadly ocean creatures are far smaller and much more difficult to see. The blue-ringed octopus and the stonefish are two of the most poisonous animals in the world, but they are small and perfectly camouflaged. Some animals have learnt to benefit from the ocean's assassins, but most just steer clear!

Lethal stone This is one stone you do not want to step on. The well-camouflaged stonefish carries deadly poisons, called neurotoxins, in the spines along its back. Its sting is strong enough to kill a human.

Toxic tentacles The Portuguese man-of-war is a floating death trap for small, unsuspecting sea creatures such as fish and shrimp. Its tentacles, which are usually about 10 metres long, deliver venom via harpoon-like stinging cells called nematocysts.

Ocean killer The blue-ringed octopus is the most deadly sea creature in the world. It is only 12–20 centimetres long, but its bite can kill a human in minutes.

Behind anemone lines

Clownfish and sea anemones have a symbiotic relationship, which means each benefits from the other. The anemone's stinging tentacles protect the clownfish from predators, and the clownfish's excretions, or waste, provide nutrients to the anemone.

The clownfish are immune to the sea anemone's poison, so they can live safely within its tentacles.

Armed and dangerous When hunting, the cuttlefish will sometimes put on a mesmerizing display of patterns and colours along its tentacles to attract prey, before striking out with paralysing venom.

Warrior snail This seemingly innocent cone shell packs a powerful weapon: a radula, or mouthpart, that injects a dose of venom into its prey that is strong enough to kill or paralyse it.

Snakes alive!

Slithering, hissing, secretive and stealthy, snakes understandably make many of us quake with fear. But snakes are also fascinating creatures. They have well-developed senses and the ability to survive and thrive in all sorts of environments – whether in water or on land, desert or rainforest, mountainous regions or flat plains.

Lightning strike
The golden eyelash viper waits in a tree and lashes out swiftly with a venomous bite. Its horny 'eyelashes' protect its eyes as it moves through vegetation.

Super sensitive A snake's senses are finely tuned to help it locate and hunt prey. It also has something called a Jacobson's organ on the roof of its mouth, which enables it to analyse chemicals picked up by its flicking, forked tongue.

Special heat-sensitive pits behind the snake's nostrils help it locate prey.

The fangs are hinged so they can fold back into the snake's mouth.

The tongue takes samples of particles in the environment and passes information to the brain.

Animal facts

❶ Snakes do not have external ears. Instead, they read vibrations using their inner ears.

❷ Snake charmers do not hypnotize snakes with music, as snakes cannot hear it! Rather, the snake responds to the swaying motion of the flute.

❸ Sea kraits can stay underwater for up to one hour.

Water snakes

There are two types of water-dwelling snakes: semi-aquatic sea kraits and true sea snakes. Sea kraits lay their eggs on land, while true sea snakes live in the water and bear live young.

Sea snakes can close their nostrils to keep out water, and have paddle-like tails to help them swim.

How do snakes 'see' their prey in the dark?

Strict diet The African egg-eating snake eats only eggs. It swallows the egg whole and breaks it using bony protrusions, or lumps, in its throat. Then it drains the egg and regurgitates the shell.

A: *By sensing temperature changes in the air around them.*

Spotlight on

rattlesnakes

The western diamondback rattlesnake can grow up to 1.5 metres long.

In the world of snakes, there is no clearer warning signal than the buzz of a rattlesnake's tail. Rattlesnakes are generally very well camouflaged in their environment, but if danger looms too close, they let their tails do the talking. All rattlesnakes have a venomous bite that can stun or kill prey within seconds.

Rough diamond Of the 33 species of rattlesnakes in the world, the diamondback is the biggest and most dangerous. It strikes with lightning speed and injects venom that destroys tissue and blood vessels.

Anatomy of a rattle

A rattlesnake's tail is made of a number of hollow, hard shells, or rings. When the snake shakes its tail, the rings knock against each other, creating a rattling sound.

Each time a rattlesnake sheds its skin, a new layer of hollow shells is formed.

The rattlesnake shakes its tail to frighten off predators or distract them from its venomous fangs while it prepares to strike.

Fangs swing forwards when the rattlesnake opens its mouth to bite.

Ambush predator

A rattlesnake strikes with incredible speed, using its coiled, muscular body as a launching pad. Its head bursts forward and quickly delivers a large dose of venom via its fangs.

A protruding windpipe helps the snake breathe while it feeds on its prey.

Venomous mammals

There are nearly 5,000 mammal species in the world, and yet barely a dozen of them are venomous. Scientists are not sure why there are so few. Perhaps it is because they have evolved other effective methods of defence and attack. Whatever the reason, these are rare and special mammals indeed.

Animal facts

1 The solenodon is one of the most endangered mammals in the world.

2 Skunks and polecats release a toxic, foul-smelling substance from near their anus when threatened. It can cause skin irritation and blindness.

3 The slow loris spreads toxin on to the fur of its young, to protect them from predators.

This sharp spur is connected to a venom gland in the platypus's leg.

Shrewd customer
The Eurasian water shrew is one of two species of shrews known to inject venom via their saliva. This weapon comes in handy when taking down larger prey, such as fish or frogs.

Webbed warrior The platypus may appear harmless, with its furry body and ducklike bill, but it is actually a fierce fighter, with a venomous spur behind its webbed back feet that can inflict a paralysing sting.

Nasty biter

The solenodon, a ratlike creature that is found only in Cuba, lives in burrows and hunts at night. Hidden within its impressively long snout is a fierce set of teeth that delivers a venomous bite.

The long, flexible snout is perfect for poking into small cracks and crevices in search of a tasty meal.

Venomous saliva comes through one of the solenodon's teeth in its lower jaw.

The solenodon hunts at night for insects, earthworms and small invertebrates, immobilizing them with venom before devouring them.

Poisoned elbows The slow loris has an unusual method of poisoning its attackers: glands in its elbows produce a brown toxin, which it licks and mixes with its saliva. This makes its bite venomous!

What is a mole's most powerful sense?

Food stash If a mole catches more earthworms than it can eat, it paralyses them with toxin in its saliva. It then stores the live worms in an underground 'kitchen' until it is hungry again.

A: Its sense of smell.

Poisonous defence

Some animals are armed with a secret defensive weapon – poison! With a bite or even just a touch, they can release enough venom to immobilize, stun or kill an attacker. Their poison comes in many different forms, from toxic feathers and skin to stinging hairs and deadly secretions.

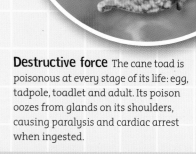

Destructive force The cane toad is poisonous at every stage of its life: egg, tadpole, toadlet and adult. Its poison oozes from glands on its shoulders, causing paralysis and cardiac arrest when ingested.

Acid attack Behind the puss moth caterpillar's charming and colourful costume lies a sinister defensive weapon: it sprays formic acid into the face of its attacker.

Why does the harmless viceroy butterfly mimic the colours and patterns of the monarch butterfly?

Poison feathers
The pitohui, which is found in New Guinea, is the only known poisonous bird in the world. The skin and feathers of some species, including this hooded pitohui, contain powerful toxins.

Warning colours The dazzling pattern on this blue-and-black poison-arrow frog is typical of the species, and warns would-be attackers to keep away. These frogs come in all the colours of the rainbow.

Killer appetite Poison-arrow frogs, such as the yellow-headed poison-arrow frog, eat a special diet of arthropods to keep up their toxicity levels. Some tribes of Central and South America coat their arrow tips with the frogs' poison.

Animal facts

1 The non-venomous tiger keelback snake eats toxic toads and uses their poison to protect itself.

2 Doctors sometimes use the modified venom of rattlesnakes and vipers to treat strokes and heart attacks in humans.

3 The most poisonous frog in the world is the golden poison-arrow frog. A small droplet of its poison is enough to kill up to 20 humans!

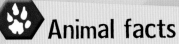

Milkweed plant

Deadly diet Monarch butterflies lay their eggs on milkweed plants as food for monarch caterpillars to eat. Milkweed contains toxins that make the adult butterflies poisonous if eaten.

A: *To trick predators into thinking that it is poisonous.*

Spitters and squirters

The element of surprise gives animals a supremely useful defensive edge when faced with an attacker. Some animals squirt, spray, regurgitate and fire all sorts of weird and wonderful substances from different parts of their body – catching their attackers off-guard so they can make a quick getaway.

Stomach bomb
Southern giant petrels, like all albatrosses and petrels, extract oil from food and store it in their stomach. They use the oil for energy, to feed their young or to regurgitate onto potential attackers.

Stinky spray When provoked, a skunk first raises its tail and stamps its feet as a warning. Then it emits a foul-smelling spray from glands in its rear, straight into its attacker's face.

Blood explosion Regal horned lizards have a bizarre method of defence: they squirt blood from behind their eyes to confuse predators. The squirt can reach up to 1.2 metres and contains fluids that cause irritation.

What shimmering fabric is made from the saliva of a certain caterpillar?

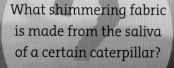

Explosive attack When threatened, a bombardier beetle fires a spray of boiling-hot, noxious fumes and fluid from a chamber in its abdomen. The mixture is so explosive that it makes a bang.

The **spitting spider** traps flies with streams of sticky, paralysing venom.

A: Silk, woven from the cocoon of the silkworm caterpillar.

Glossary

abdomen the part of an animal's body that contains the digestive system and organs of reproduction

ambush the act of attacking by surprise from a concealed or camouflaged position

anaesthetic a substance that causes loss of sensitivity in an animal, either by numbing a small area of its body or by rendering it unconscious

anatomy the detailed structure of any part of an animal or plant

appendage any part of an animal that branches off from its main body

aquatic living or growing in water

arthropod a type of animal with a segmented body and jointed legs whose skeleton is on the outside of its body. Spiders and ants are arthropods.

asphyxiate to stop the intake of oxygen and release of carbon dioxide through breathing; to choke

camouflage body colours, patterns or shapes that help an animal blend in with and stay hidden in its natural surroundings

canine teeth four pointed teeth, one on each side of each jaw, sitting between the front incisors and the side molars. Not all animals have canine teeth.

canopy the upper leafy branches of a tree or trees

carapace a shell-like cover on the back and sometimes front of an animal

cardiac arrest the stopping of blood pumping to and from the heart. Electric shocks, asphyxia and some poisons can cause cardiac arrest.

carnivore an animal that eats the flesh of other animals

chameleon a type of lizard that can change the colour of its skin to match its environment

colony a group of animals or plants of the same kind living together

congregate to gather together, often in a large group

constrictor a snake that kills by coiling around its prey

crustacean a type of animal, usually aquatic, whose body is covered by a hard outer covering, or shell. Lobsters, crabs and shrimps are crustaceans.

decoy an artificial bait or lure, designed to entice an animal towards or away from something

dorsal describes a part of an animal's back

duct in an animal, a duct is a tube or canal through which a bodily fluid, such as a snake's venom, travels

excretions waste substances released by a plant or animal, such as urine, sweat or faeces

fibrous made up of a number of separate threadlike pieces

gland a part of the body that makes and releases (secretes) useful substances

herbivore an animal that eats only plants

hierarchy a system of ranking things in a certain order

impenetrable incapable of being broken into or entered

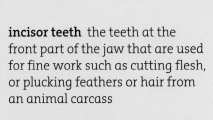

incisor teeth the teeth at the front part of the jaw that are used for fine work such as cutting flesh, or plucking feathers or hair from an animal carcass

ingest to put food into the body

invertebrates animals without backbones, such as jellyfish, spiders (whose skeletons are on the outside) and insects

keratin a type of protein found in human and animal skin and hair, as well as claws, nails, hooves, horns and feathers

krill tiny, shrimplike sea creatures that live in large numbers in Arctic and Antarctic waters

mammals a group of animals that have hair or fur, are warm-blooded and feed their young with milk

mandible the lower part of the jaw

masquerade a disguise

microsurgery surgery that is performed on extremely small parts of the body, such as veins and arteries

mimicry the act of mimicking or imitating something else

noxious harmful to health

order a subdivision of plants and animals

parasite a plant or animal that survives by extracting nutrients from another plant or animal

pectoral describes a part of an animal's chest

pedipalps appendages near the mouth of an arachnid such as a spider or scorpion, used as weapons or to help with feeding

plumage a bird's feathers

pod a collective term for animals, usually seals or whales

pores tiny openings in an animal's skin, or on the surface of a leaf

predator an animal that survives by hunting, killing and eating other animals

prehistoric belonging to a period before recorded history

prey an animal or animals that are hunted, killed and eaten by other animals

primates mammals belonging to the order Primates. Examples include humans, monkeys, chimpanzees, and gorillas.

protrusion something that projects from, or sticks out of, something else

raptor a bird of prey, such as an eagle, hawk or owl

reflex an immediate, often involuntary, physical response to a stimulus

regurgitate to bring back food that has been fully or partially digested

remnant a small remaining trace of something

savannah a type of landscape characterized by flatness and sparse vegetation dominated by grasses. These landscapes are usually found in hot places, such as Africa.

school a group of fish

spurs sharp, clawlike structures on the legs of some birds and mammals

urethra the tube through which urine passes from the bladder

versatile capable of doing different tasks easily

vertebrates animals with backbones, such as humans, dogs and whales

Index

The publisher thanks Puddingburn Publishing Services for the index.

Credits

Key tl=top left; t=top; tc=top centre; tr=top right; cl=centre left; c=centre; cr=centre right; bl=bottom left; bc=bottom centre; br=bottom right; bg = background

CBCD = Kodak Photo Disc; CBT = Corbis; GI = Getty Images; iS = istockphoto.com; NHPA = Photoshot; SH = Shutterstock; TPL = photolibrary.com

PHOTOGRAPHS
Front Cover br, cr CBT;
Back Cover tl iS;
1tr iS; **2**bl iS; **3**c CBT; br iS; **4**cl iS; **5**tr GI; **6-7**c CBT; **8-9**bg iS; **11**bg CBCD; br CBT; tc iS; tl SH; **12**bl, tr iS; **16**bl, br, tr iS; tr SH; **16-17**c iS; **17**tc CBT; tl iS; **18**tl iS; br, cl, cr TPL; **19**c GI; tc TPL; **20**c TPL; **20-21**bc, tc GI; **21**tl GI; br iS; **22-23**c CBT; **24**bl CBT; **28**bl CBT; cl GI; **29**tl CBT; **30**cr GI; **32**bc, cl, tr iS; **32-33**cr iS; **33**tc iS; **34-35**c CBT; **36**br, cl, tr iS; **38**tr iS; **40**bl SH; **41**tl SH; **42**bl, c iS; **42-43**bg iS; **43**cr, tc iS; **44**tr NHPA; **44-45**bg iS; **45**cl, tr CBT; br iS; **48-49**c CBT; **51**tl iS; **52**tr GI; **52-53**bg iS; **53**br GI; **54**cl, tc iS; **56-57**bc GI; bg iS; **57**cl CBT; br iS; **58**cl CBT; **58-59**bg, tc iS; **58**tr iS; bc NHPA; **59**tl, tr iS; **60**c CBT; tr iS; **62**tl CBCD; tl NHPA

ILLUSTRATIONS
Peter Bull Art Studios 27br, 47t; Leonello Calvetti 14t, 24r; Barry Croucher/The Art Agency 14bl, 37, 54-55; Christer Eriksson 9, 10tl, 17r, 25; 41cr, 47; Gary Hanna/The Art Agency 26-27, 53t; Steve Hobbs 41t, 59, 61; Ian Jackson/The Art Agency 8bl, 10 bl, 10b, 40b, 50t, tr; David Kirshner 52-53; MBA Studios 26, 28-29; Terry Pastor/The Art Agency 60bl; Sandra Pond/The Art Agency 57tr; Mick Posen/The Art Agency 8tr, 14-15, 40cl, 46l, 50-51; Kevin Stead 21r, 56; Claude Thivierge/Contact Jupiter 11t, 11tr; Kim Thompson/Kingpin 17t, 42-43; Guy Troughton 44